PhilanthropyRoundtable

Uniform
Champions

A Wise Giver's Guide to Excellent Assistance for Veterans

By Thomas Meyer

Published by The Philanthropy Roundtable, 1120 20th Street NW, Suite 550 South, Washington, D.C. 20036

Free copies of this book are available to qualified donors. To learn more, or to order more copies, call (202) 822-8333, e-mail main@PhilanthropyRoundtable.org, or visit PhilanthropyRoundtable.org. Printed and e-book versions are available from major online booksellers. A PDF may be downloaded at no charge at PhilanthropyRoundtable.org.

Cover: istockphoto.com / filo

ISBN 978-0-9892202-8-6
LCCN 2017933362

First printing, March 2017

Current Wise Giver's Guides from The Philanthropy Roundtable

Karl Zinsmeister, *series editor*

For all current and future titles, visit PhilanthropyRoundtable.org/guidebook

TABLE OF CONTENTS

PREFACE

Support for veterans and military families is an evolving field of American charitable assistance, and The Philanthropy Roundtable is proud to have been an early leader in its development. We established a dedicated program in this area in 2012 and hired Thomas Meyer to advise and guide the many donors expressing interest in taking up this work. In 2013 we published *Serving Those Who Served*, a guidebook for donors that was one of the first methodical assessments of the work most needed in this field, and the charities offering promising services. Many conferences, articles, and extended individual consultations have followed.

Five years on, we are pleased to publish this new guidebook—which profiles more than 15 exemplary givers who are helping former servicemembers launch productive, healthy, and happy civilian lives. Each donor is profiled in some depth. Their stories will help you better understand the real needs of veterans, and what hard experience has indicated to be the best ways of helping them. The comments of these leading philanthropists throw valuable light on the satisfactions, pitfalls, and high potential of this corner of philanthropic service.

This guidebook also includes a collection of vital statistics that donors can consult to inform their giving. There are many myths and sentimental misnomers swirling around the question of what today's new veterans most require as they enter civilian life. The factual information at the back of this volume will help you develop a clearer picture of the true needs—and potential—of these impressive men and women. It also shows what government agencies are doing for veterans. Much of that public assistance is ineffective, and this book is full of suggestions on ways to fill gaps so that new veterans will thrive.

We are grateful to the Anschutz Foundation for being a pioneer funder of The Philanthropy Roundtable's work to aid veterans. The Anschutz family was crucial in helping us found this program and build it into the nation's best of its kind. Christian Anschutz, who has led his family's effort in this area, has written the introduction to this book.

We also want to acknowledge the following funders for generous, timely, indispensable support of our organization's services for veterans: the Diana Davis Spencer Foundation, Kovner Foundation, Laura and John Arnold Foundation, Daniels Fund, Milbank Foundation, Harry and Jeanette Weinberg Foundation, Marcus Foundation, J. A. and Kathryn

Albertson Foundation, Morgridge Family Foundation, Ahmanson Foundation, Heinz Endowments, Wilf Family Foundations, Paul E. Singer Foundation, Lynde & Harry Bradley Foundation, F. M. Kirby Foundation, AIG, I. A. O'Shaughnessy Foundation, Achelis & Bodman Foundations, USAA Foundation, and Cohen Veterans Network.

We thank researcher Ric Arthur for joining Thomas Meyer in interviews with some of the philanthropists in this book and turning some of that information into background drafts. Researcher Ashley May made similar contributions.

The Philanthropy Roundtable exists to help American donors pursue their charitable goals as effectively as possible. If there is some way we can assist you in refining your giving, elevating fellow men and women, and strengthening our free society, please let us know.

And let us know at main@PhilanthropyRoundtable.org or 202.822.8333 if you have colleagues you would like to receive copies of this book. (Print and electronic versions are also available at major online bookstores.)

Adam Meyerson
President
The Philanthropy Roundtable

INTRODUCTION

The Anschutz family recognizes the service and sacrifice of our men and women in uniform, and realizes that if it were not for their service, there would be no private enterprise, no personal freedom, and no opportunity to pass along the many blessings of living in a free and prosperous nation! Because of that desire to recognize those who have risked their lives in the service of our country, The Anschutz Foundation helped launch The Philanthropy Roundtable's philanthropic effort in support of our veterans. When doing so, we began with several key assumptions. These insights were missing from many charitable supports for veterans at that time—which is why we supported the advisory effort to help donors improve their giving. Here are examples of some of the central premises we began with:

- **Veterans are assets to be built up, not liabilities to be fixed.** The vast majority of veterans adjust smoothly to civilian life—often because of the responsibilities and even stresses they had to cope with during their military service. Young veterans who are struggling often just need an intelligently targeted boost, and then they are able to contribute to the nation's economic and civic strength the rest of their lives.
- **Incentives matter.** Veterans, as you will see in the statistical section of this book, are well above average in most measures of character, education, skill, and human potential. But every person responds to the incentives society offers them. If donors and nonprofits simply give things to veterans instead of challenging them and helping them become their best selves, these young men and women are at risk of becoming dependents, or languishing well below their potential—just like anyone else who is told he is entitled, or broken, or not responsible for his life. Donors who want veterans to thrive should help them become self-reliant.
- **Veterans are not a separate species.** Very often, the charitable organizations that will be most helpful to veterans are those that are excellent in ministering to other populations. Whether it is health care, job placement, or education, it may be most effective for a philanthropist to

help an existing champion in that category extend itself a bit to fold veterans into its mission, instead of always creating a veteran-specific organization.

- **Focus your attention and your spending.** The best donors and organizations are generally those that pick one or two specialties and focus intently on them. It can be tempting for donors to try to fund every potential need a veteran may face. Usually it will make more of a difference if you master just a few offerings and do them well.

You are about to read a collection of real experiences by savvy, leading donors, laboring across a wide range of issues and places. Their work is some of the most excellent being done for veterans today. Once you have absorbed the practical lessons they've learned, and glimpsed the strategies they apply to make sure they hit their targets, you will be well equipped to excel in this important philanthropic work too.

This is a young field in private giving. It's one where you can leave your own proud philanthropic legacy. In the process, you will bolster your nation, your community, and some of the most worthy men and women in America.

Christian Anschutz
Director, The Anschutz Foundation
Managing Director, Western Development Group

MAKING THE CASE FOR PHILANTHROPY FOR VETERANS

Charitable donations and programs for veterans and military families have been one of the fastest-growing corners of philanthropy over the last decade. Yet despite new and increased commitments (lots of them profiled in this book), many donors have remained on the sidelines. In doing so, they miss out on some of the greatest philanthropic opportunities in the country, and an opportunity to give back to a crucial population on which American prosperity is built. Let's look at a few of the arguments sometimes cited as reasons not to extend philanthropy to veterans.

Myth 1: The government already has this covered!
$167 billion and 350,000 full-time employees—that's how big the U.S. Department of Veterans Affairs was in 2016. And those figures don't include the billions spent by the Departments of Defense, Labor, and Health and Human Services, plus the Social Security Administration, to provide unemployment benefits, job training, civilian disability pay, and housing, among other forms of government support provided to veterans. Glance at these numbers, and one might conclude that veterans' needs are so well-funded by the government that there couldn't possibly be any need for private philanthropy.

It's certainly true that the V.A. is richly funded. It has been the fastest growing major federal agency for most of a decade. But unfortunately the issue is by no means covered.

The government is regularly embroiled in scandal and backlog. In the last few years alone, the agency accumulated a mountain of unprocessed disability claims that at one point peaked at over 600,000 cases. Wait times for medical appointments at V.A. health centers around the country have often stretched to ridiculous periods. There have been systemic problems with falsifying patient records. There are no doubt some excellent clinicians, public servants, and facilities, but there have also been persistent incidents of negligence, infection, and death in V.A. health-care facilities. Despite the billions of taxpayer dollars spent on employment and job training programs, their quality is often low, and young veterans have less success than civilian peers at landing suitable work after service. Even the V.A.'s National Cemetery Administration has struggled, mislabeling remains and grave sites for veterans buried on its land. Service breakdowns of all sorts continue to emerge from the bureaucracies charged with serving veterans, despite Congress throwing heaps of money into the V.A. budget.

Even when the V.A. functions as planned, it (like many large institutions) has a hard time adapting quickly to the needs of the day. Most of the V.A.'s health resources go to everyday geriatric medical care, not military-specific illnesses and injuries for those who left service recently. Its disability compensation system ($68 billion in 2016) uses WWII-era labor market expectations to cut monthly checks to veterans based on antiquated and unchanging medical diagnoses, creating perverse incentives that discourage recovery, employment, and independence among the injured. There is such a huge weight of special interest groups and powerful lobbies hanging on existing agencies and procedures that it is politically, bureaucratically, and legally almost impossible to change the way programs operate or services are delivered. Old procedures stay in place practically in perpetuity.

And then there's the fact that there are many needs that no government agency, however well-managed, is equipped to address. Building a sense of community and mutual support among veterans, offering emotional sustenance to their families, creating mentoring relationships with successful neighbors—these are things no bureaucratic agency is likely to be able to accomplish. Yet they are some of the most important needs today in helping recent servicemembers make a successful transition to civilian life.

Myth 2: Philanthropy is too small in scale to make a dent!

Philanthropic services contrast sharply with what the V.A. provides, on almost every level. Most charitable budgets are orders of magnitude smaller than what the V.A. spends. But the philanthropic efforts are far less regimented, far more personal. They can be much more innovative and experimental. They can be vastly more efficient, and accountable—being subject to rapid reform or shutdown if they fail to meet veterans' needs. Philanthropy thus has a vital role to play in supporting veterans and military families.

Smaller budgets require focus and carefully thought-out procedures that have been proven to work. That's why funders like the Call of Duty Endowment are able to place veterans in good jobs for less than $600 each—a fraction of the cost of government programs. Decentralized problem-solving means that the Marcus Foundation can support a range of clinical and non-traditional programs that cater to the individual needs of veterans with mental-health challenges and brain injuries, and try all sorts of new approaches to see which work best. Nimble funders like the J. A. and Kathryn Albertson Foundation are bringing high-quality charitable services to veterans in geographic regions where literally no services currently exist. Other donors, like the Cohen Veterans Network, keep an eagle eye on service usage and quickly reallocate resources when clients require greater or fewer mental-health supports than expected in a particular area, allowing a given level of funding to be used with hyper precision and efficiency.

Myth 3: We can't fund veterans because they're not mentioned in our charter!

Very few philanthropic groups have any explicit mention of support for veterans in their charters. But there are lots of new or evolving charitable needs that were unmentioned when typical charities were set up. How many foundations have HIV/AIDS, or cybersecurity, or Zika, or methamphetamine abuse mentioned in their charters? That doesn't block donors from entering new kinds of work when needs arise. Most philanthropies focus on specific geographies, or broad issue areas like education, health, scientific research, or job training. Much-needed assistance for veterans can be implemented under any number of headings.

Many top nonprofits that didn't previously serve veterans have come to recognize them as important constituents, and seamlessly adjusted their programs to better serve them. Donors ought to consider the same reasoning. The Harry and Jeanette Weinberg Foundation, for instance, an influential $2 billion entity that operates nationally and internationally with special interests in topics like work, disability, and poverty, realized it was already funding programs that serve veterans in a number of its portfolios. So it recently developed a coherent veterans' strategy that organized and linked those offerings to make them even more effective and accessible to former servicemembers.

Many of the most trenchant issues that veterans face today are subsets of problems that our society faces more broadly. For example, numerous agencies and private businesses are seeing dramatic increases in the number of working-age individuals filing for disability compensation. Veterans have lots of civilian company in this alarming problem of comparatively young males dropping out of the workforce due to foolish incentive structures.

Likewise, our concerns over veterans piling up burdensome student debt in pursuit of degrees that don't land them jobs is part of a wider problem in higher education. When it comes to health, rising alarm over syndromes like concussion, prescription drug misuse, behavioral disorders, suicide, obesity, and lower back pain apply to millions of Americans, regardless of whether they served in uniform. Fixes developed for any of these challenges facing veterans will also have positive spillover effects for millions of other Americans. That's why the Laura and John Arnold Foundation, for one more example, is investing in improved outcome assessment and program accountability in services created for veterans—because things we learn helping them will be transferable to many other sectors, speeding the cause of evidence-based problem-solving that is a deep Arnold passion.

Myth 4: I've heard stories about ineffective or fraudulent or ineffective vets' groups—it's impossible to separate the good from the bad!

Donors are properly anxious to avoid phony or ineffective charities. This is something any donor has to guard against in every sector. Thousands of nonprofits claim to be serving veterans and military personnel. Some have been shown to be poor operations. Many share similar names. How is a donor to avoid bad apples?

Downright fraudulent groups exist, but they are very rare. A much more serious issue is mediocrity. Even the savviest funders will make missteps if they are trying new things in new fields with new service providers. The key is simply to assess carefully, adjust quickly when there are disappointments, and move on. For instance, after seeing no impact from one of its early grants as a pioneer investor in veterans' causes, the Call of Duty Endowment took a step back and came up with a new grant-making process. This procedure is now so rigorous it can show exactly how many dollars it takes a particular nonprofit to put a veteran in a job, every quarter.

The best donors start funding small, and *assume* there are going to be hiccups and failures. As they work out the kinks, they expand the successful programs. The Cohen Veterans Network, for instance, started with one site that took a couple of years to perfect. Once they had the model down, they began to spread it at breakneck speed. One of the reasons many ambitious donors enjoy philanthropy for veterans is because it is a young field where the practitioners are still learning how to best serve the population—and thus offers many opportunities to pioneer, innovate, and lead in the search for better ways of delivering philanthropic services.

As you work to separate attractive veterans organizations and programs from those that don't appeal to you, ask yourself some simple questions. Is this problem actually a result of military service? Do veterans experience it more often or more intensely than nonveterans? Are there other resources (particularly generous V.A. benefits) that already address this need in effective ways? Are the people who benefit from this likely to succeed regardless of this program? Is this a cost-effective way of solving the problem, and is there evidence that it actually works? What kind of behavior does the program reward or discourage? Just as in other areas of charitable service, you will soon become comfortable in separating the sheep from the goats.

Myth 5: Our wars are winding down, so there won't be much need for veterans' philanthropy in the future!

No one can read the tea leaves of foreign affairs accurately enough to predict what the members of our military will be doing in future years. But even if you could, you'd be missing the point. Every year, about a quarter of a million Americans move from military service to veteran status. That means new jobs, new communities, new financial situations, new social networks, new health-care needs, and new identities. Maintaining an all-volunteer military means a constant turnover in personnel regardless of whether the nation is at war.

Most vets transition well to civilian life and become potent assets to their communities. With education and civilian work experience, they help fuel our economy, contribute to the tax base, and solidify their own financial status. Their leadership skills often allow them to become very useful to their companies, their hometowns, and their nation. Several philanthropies like the J. A. and Kathryn Albertson Foundation and the Heinz Endowments are already using veterans as assets for solving entrenched problems in their regional communities. When we allow transitions to civilian life to go poorly, both veterans and our country lose out.

Think different

Like veterans' benefits, education is an area that was completely dominated by government for generations. We all agree that public education is a national imperative, and that when it is done right, individuals, communities, and the economy all flourish. When it is botched, everyone suffers.

Every year, government at various levels spends hundreds of billions on education. Traditionally, K–12 education was a government monopoly in most of the country. Despite the many excellent and committed individuals working in the system, that monopoly, like most monopolies, developed serious problems: weak incentives for improvement, a systemic lack of accountability, and capture by strong political constituencies that hamstrung the system's flexibility and capacities to experiment and modernize. The quality of services declined, while costs skyrocketed.

The trajectory of public education in America is in some ways mirrored by the provision of veterans' services over recent decades. But in the early 1990s, their stories diverged. Students in some of our urban public schools got an escape hatch—charter schools. These public schools operated by nonprofit entities must meet the same educational standards that conventional schools do, but they have far more autonomy in structuring the school year, hiring and compensating teachers, experimenting with teaching styles, building a school culture, and so forth. Teachers and schools that allow student performance to slip are regularly shut down.

Applying the twin principles of flexibility and accountability, great philanthropists like John Walton, Don Fisher, and Bill and Melinda Gates launched thousands of inventive schools and instructional models. Some of them immediately performed marvelously. Some had to be adjusted and re-tuned. Some didn't perform and were summarily shut down. But ultimately, this accountable, meritocratic environment yielded dramatically better outcomes for millions of students who had been failed by traditional schooling. This has been one of the great triumphs of private philanthropy over the last generation.

Our system of services for veterans is ripe for a similar philanthropically inspired upgrade. The V.A. medical system has received much notoriety for failures in care. But plenty of other corners of public support for veterans are also in dire need of rethinking. The V.A.'s employment programs are tremendously expensive and don't produce the good results of top nonprofits. V.A. disability benefits are built on grossly outdated understandings of our economy, and create perverse incentives for counterproductive behavior.

V.A. scandals have mushroomed in exactly the same decade and a half that the agency's budget has *tripled*. Clearly more of the same approach is not what veterans need today. We need fresh thinking and new ways of delivering services. Those are areas where private philanthropy excels— as you'll learn in the chapters that follow.

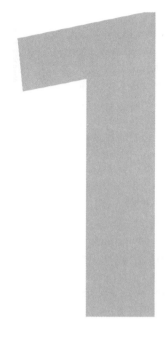

A Gamer Puts Vets to Work: The Call of Duty Endowment separates potent nonprofits from also-rans

"Call of Duty Endowment" doesn't immediately evoke thoughts of a hard-headed nonprofit that matches veterans with meaningful work. Some parents reading this are more likely to blame *Call of Duty* for the unwillingness of a teenager to get a job—because it is one of America's most popular video games. Launched in 2003, the franchise has in fact become one of the most successful entertainment ventures of any kind in the world—beloved among many for its cinematic quality and because it allows players to embody military personnel on screen as they complete different missions in conflicts dating back to World War II. Following a strategy of "narrow but deep," *Call of Duty's* parent company, Activision Blizzard, has released 24 variations on the theme and made a lot of money in the process. The company decided it wanted to plow some of its profits into helping real-life warfighters, so it set up a philanthropy for veterans called the Call of Duty Endowment, or CODE, and quickly turned it into one of the savviest givers in this field.

A large part of the success of both the company and the philanthropic spinoff comes from leadership at the top. Bobby Kotick has served as CEO of his game company since 1991. He guided it through dangerously competitive waters to its current success.

Then he had an experience that added a whole new priority to his life. He spent a few days as a guest aboard an aircraft carrier operating off the California coast. He got to experience takeoffs and landings, battle drills, and the round-the-clock competence of an anthill of hard-working servicemembers. This experience inspired him to look for ways to help former servicemembers as they moved into civilian life. As Kotick tells it,

> The Call of Duty Endowment was born in 2009 from a conversation I had with former V.A. Secretary Jim Nicholson in 2007. I mentioned to him that a philanthropic foundation was planning to build a performing arts center on the grounds of the V.A. facility in West Los Angeles to benefit veterans. His response was, "That's stupid. Our real priorities are finding them jobs and improving their health care."

Nicholson had a point. In 2009, newly demobilized veterans were entering an economy reeling from the worst recession since the 1930s. The reported unemployment rate for post-9/11 veterans was well above the civilian rate, and younger veterans were having the hardest time of anyone. There were plenty of vet-friendly employers looking to hire, and an ample supply of ready-to-work veterans. But they were having a hard time finding each another.

The problem was clear to Kotick. But solutions seemed to be in short supply. Government spent a lot of money on sprawling jobs programs for transitioning servicemembers, but with little evidence of success, and no eye for the bottom line. Meanwhile, many employers were relying on hiring managers with little experience of military life and no idea how to judge the merits of a veteran applicant. Philanthropy could remedy this mismatch.

Kotick decided to fund organizations that bridge the gap between employers and veterans. He launched CODE toward the end of 2009, and it has since helped more than 25,000 veterans find high-quality jobs. The endowment's successes have been built on strategic discipline, a willingness to learn from early mistakes, and years of rigorous process.

Finding the way
To get the ball rolling, Kotick and his staff launched the endowment as an independent 501c3 and hired an advocacy and marketing organization to take care of grantmaking. The company set aside some initial funding and asked interested senior executives at Activision Blizzard to volunteer time to help steer the ship.

> CODE's average donation is now half a million dollars, as opposed to $50,000 in its early years. "Our grants are ten times bigger because we're ten times more confident."

At that time, there were no examples of what a top-shelf employment organization for veterans should look like. And there wasn't much information available from the charities doing this work about how their groups performed or were managed. Generous donors were looking to make grants, and high-quality nonprofits were looking for funding, but they had no easy way of identifying each other. Under these conditions, the endowment did its best to distribute funding to organizations that seemed to have the right intentions. Between 2009 and 2011, CODE offered many small- and medium-size grants to groups that said they could help veterans find jobs.

Though made with the best of intentions, the board became uneasy about its inability to assess the outcomes from these initial grants. And the very biggest grant it made—$100,000 to a prominent organization—was a clear bust. When CODE asked the leadership of that organization what sort of impact its dollars had, the manager couldn't begin to answer the question. It had nothing to show for the resources it had expended, and didn't even have a firm grasp on where the money had gone.

This sounded alarm bells for Kotick and the other Activision Blizzard executives running CODE. Although it hurt to know this initial investment had been squandered, Kotick knew that if they could learn useful things from the failure, the experience would not be wasted. He asked his team to figure out how it could feel more confident in its investments, and CODE paused all new grantmaking until a better strategy was in place.

Narrow but deep

Kotick realized he needed to bring on a full-time executive to lead the endowment—someone with good business judgment and a strong desire to help veterans. After 12 months of searching he hired Dan Goldenberg. A Navy Reservist with a decade of business consulting under his belt, Goldenberg's favorite method for solving problems was by solving *processes*. That seemed to Kotick to be the right approach.

Goldenberg began his work in an excellent position: Kotick didn't expect him to make any grants until he was confident he had the right approach. This gave Goldenberg breathing room to survey the field, meet the players, and determine how CODE could make the greatest impact. He started by breaking down the various stages, activities, milestones, and failure points in the employment process. He pinpointed specific inefficiencies in the labor market—lack of exposure to a range of careers, poor assessment of veteran interests, not understanding how people with military experience and training would fit in various industries, problems in translating military experience to civilian work, weaknesses in job search methods and networking, and difficulties in adapting to certain norms of civilian work, among other factors. Goldenberg then assessed how well each of those challenges were being met by current programs, where philanthropic funding could be a helpful tool, and what kinds of assistance best fit CODE's philanthropic mission. Where those factors overlapped—high-need, not served, open to nonprofit intervention—CODE would plant its flag.

Within four months, Dan had identified his targets. CODE would support organizations that helped veterans conduct realistic career assessments and then showed them how to do the practical things necessary to land a job offer. CODE chose not to fund indirect approaches like mentorship programs or educating hiring managers on the capacities of vets. The group's tightened focus dictated how it would judge funding proposals. And it showed what measurements to look for: job placements made, cost per placement, and quality of placements (judged by salary and job-retention rates).

Goldenberg believed CODE had better chances of success if it funded fewer but better organizations. "Diluting resources among every worthwhile need would make it that much harder to measure whether or not the endowment was having an effect," he notes. He found inspiration in one of the foundational beliefs of CODE's parent company—that it is best to do one thing well than to stray into efforts that are too broad. Just as Activision Blizzard bet heavily on a small number of blockbuster hits, CODE would zero in "on veterans' employment. Not health care, not community-building, not education, not even spousal employment. We had to be very narrow."

CODE would further focus on providing the capital to help small but clearly promising organizations grow. Brand-new startups wouldn't be able to show the evidence of success or organizational stability that CODE wanted, but there were plenty of already-existing organizations out there that could demonstrate a big potential upside given some philanthropic backing. On the other end of the spectrum, CODE decided it would avoid grants to sustain current operations of groups. The endowment wanted growth candidates that could drive down the cost per job placement by grabbing economies of larger scale. Most importantly, CODE believed there was (and still is) serious unmet demand among veterans for help in finding good jobs, so it sought partners who were anxious to expand rather than just continue at current capacities.

A seal of distinction

As CODE was establishing its strategy, its demanding board pressed for procedures that would find the best value in the shortest amount of time with limited manpower. Enter Chuck Shapiro, a senior executive at Activision Blizzard who helped set up CODE and sat on its board. He specialized in conducting internal assessments of the company's business divisions—clear-eyed, information-based, business audits are the lens through which Shapiro views the world. He was shocked by how few charities for veterans had meaningful assessments for analyzing the financial health, governance, and results of their programs. No one should have to make investment decisions with so little information.

Shapiro suspected it would be possible to use a modified version of his corporate audit toolkit to assess the performance of nonprofits and compare them on similar terms. Having previously led a risk-management team at Deloitte, he reached out to his old team for advice and assistance. They helped him to develop assessments similar to the ones used in corporate America, with changes like replacing earnings measures with population numbers, price per placement, and job retention. His standard audit looks at four major categories—expenditures, program operations and outcomes, financial stability, and on-site observations.

Shapiro and Deloitte had repurposed a corporate audit for the social sector. None of this was rocket science, but it did organize information so CODE and other funders could make fair and meaningful comparisons of organizations and spot strengths and areas of concern, without leaving much room for sentimental pleas or anecdotal claims. In addition to helping develop the tool, Deloitte conducts on-site portions of each audit. Deloitte donates this work (on top of its contributions in developing the audit) as part of its corporate philanthropy.

> The nonprofit formed a partnership with Deloitte. Together they developed a detailed multi-day assessment that they now use to identify the field's most effective operators.

With this audit tool in hand, CODE now faced the necessity of convincing charities to open themselves up to this rigorous process. The Deloitte connection, Goldenberg notes, was helpful in convincing nonprofits of the credibility and fairness of the audit. The consulting firm's brand name made it easier to convince charities to undergo the process.

To further entice cooperation, Goldenberg developed the "Seal of Distinction"—a prize the endowment offers to any nonprofit submitting to and passing the audit. The seal provides public recognition, validation from a high-profile funder, and a $30,000 unrestricted grant. This carrot enabled CODE to quickly gather information on a wide range of potential grantees so they could all be compared on the same terms. Not everyone who wins a seal becomes a CODE grantee. But in opening their books, all the participating groups help improve the overall quality of philanthropy for veterans. The seal continues to be a mandatory first step for nonprofits hoping to earn large grants from CODE.

The initial application for the Seal of Distinction is just a few pages long and collects basic, concrete information on an organization's competence. If an organization can't complete the application, that indicates it isn't working at the level that CODE needs in a partner. If an organization meets the initial parameters that CODE is looking for, it becomes a semi-finalist. Deloitte then conducts a three-to-five-day on-site assessment to measure the health and productivity of the organization. Since 2011, Deloitte has conducted about 50 audits of potential grantees.

Organizations that pass full muster are awarded the Seal of Distinction. Even in cases where the endowment cannot fund an organization, Goldenberg believes the seal is very helpful to the group in raising the level of its game. "I offer short consultations even to those organizations that *don't* win, because you can't get better if you don't get feedback." In this way, CODE is improving the field and encouraging best practices in the future, one organization at a time.

Building up charities

Once an applicant organization earns the Seal of Distinction, the application process becomes a conversation between the charity and the endowment about what outcomes could be achieved for a given amount of money. Each grant is engineered so that it encourages grantees to increase the size of their operation by hiring more staff or expanding their geographical footprint to an underserved area. If Goldenberg and the potential grantee agree on a basic plan, he brings the idea to his board for consultation. If the board ratifies the proposal, CODE and the grantee put together a one- or two-page agreement that memorializes the performance commitments—and a one-year grant is made.

"If you'll notice, nowhere in our process is a requirement to send a 30-page grant request over the wall. Once an organization proves itself through the Seal of Distinction, the relationship becomes very simple, open, and transparent—based on earned trust," says Goldenberg. "At that point, it's simply about what can we do together. We look for any number of ways the endowment can help them."

Goldenberg is cognizant of the need for a mixed portfolio of organizations to meet the diverse needs of the veteran population. Reaching homeless and high-barrier veterans is a very different process, requiring markedly different capacities, than finding jobs for transitioning vets who just need a little direction. CODE is willing to support both kinds of assistance, and more, and in any part of the country.

One example of a CODE grantee is Corporate America Supports You (CASY). It has received endowment grants for four years. Since 2010, CASY has placed more than 20,000 veterans in jobs, with an average starting salary of $69,000 in 2016. The group is especially efficient at taking National Guardsmen and Reservists, who are older and generally pretty well-prepared for the civilian workforce, and connecting them quickly to employers looking to hire ex-military.

CASY uses low-cost remote coaching to help veterans discover their career options, complete short-term training, market themselves, and navigate the application and interview processes. It also works closely with employers to understand what kind of skills they need in new hires. In 2016, the endowment funded CASY with $1.4 million, enabling the charity to expand at Fort Hood in Texas (a major exit point for members of the Army).

Sometimes, rather than expanding an existing effort, CODE will ask a grantee to bring its services to a new region where there is a large veteran population and not enough help with job placement. For example: the Salvation Army Haven specializes in serving high-need veterans, those who have been homeless, addicted, or involved in crime. In 2015, the endowment helped the Salvation Army add a new Haven location in Antelope Valley, 60 miles north of Los Angeles.

Despite the difficulties of ministering to its target populations, the Haven has a 78 percent job-placement rate for enrollees, and fully 90 percent of the program's placements are still at their job after six months. Its cost per placement is higher than most of the other grantees in the CODE network, but that's because it works with more difficult clients. CODE has helped the Haven lower its costs while increasing impact. Because of the special challenges of its population, expanding and improving operations at the Haven requires different things than it does among CASY's high-functioning participants. CODE has been able to shift gears and help both groups without difficulty.

In its first few years, CODE's average grant was between $40,000 and $50,000. Today, its average donation is $400,000 to $500,000. "Right now our grants are ten times bigger because we're ten times more confident," summarizes Goldenberg. Brian Stann, CEO of grantee partner Hire Heroes USA, likes to measure his organization's progress by comparing the $10,000 CODE grant it first received in the early days to what it is getting today. In 2016, Hire Heroes USA received a $1.4 million check from the endowment.

CODE is also flexible enough to consider one-time gifts. In 2014, Easter Seals decided to expand an employment agency it runs as a social venture (matching hard-to-employ individuals to companies in need of workers) by adding a focus on veterans. Experienced coaches were linked to those needing jobs. Client companies willing to pay a fee were connected to job-ready clients produced by Easter Seals. And the coaches continued to work with their veterans throughout their employment, to make sure they transitioned well to their workplace and remained effective on the job even if challenges arose. CODE provided $250,000 in funding to help set up the Easter Seals Veteran Staffing Network. Once it was running, the network was able to bring on enough new paying companies to sustain its work using earned revenue, eliminating the need for further grant funding.

> The audit and quality-control and continual-improvement procedures of CODE have elevated the entire field of employment services for vets.

More than cutting a check

The net effects of the Call of Duty Endowment are much more than just the sum of its savvy individual grants. The audit and quality-control and continual-improvement procedures described above have helped elevate the entire field of employment services for vets. On a more micro level, CODE has had powerful effects on the nine grantee organizations that it has particularly cultivated with larger grants and extensive time and attention—helping them take important leadership roles in the field. These grantees cover a wide range of subpopulations, regions, economic niches, and philanthropic styles.

And the regular reports that its grantees provide to CODE yield extremely useful signals on the true state of the labor market for veterans. For example, the U.S. Bureau of Labor Statistics reported that 2015 saw a considerable decrease in unemployment rates for veterans. But the BLS survey samples are too small to provide reliable conclusions, and the questions are too general to provide useful information on important topics like underemployment among those who do have jobs. The fact that CODE grantees, taken together, have seen demand for employment services rise by about a quarter over the latest year has leavened the government statistic, shown that unemployment among vets is not fully solved, and helped service agencies zero in on the neediest populations.

CODE has begun to periodically convene its grantees to share information, compare notes on best practices, discuss obstacles, and brainstorm on mutually useful projects. Goldenberg convened the first of these gatherings in the spring of 2016 in Chicago. Other meetings will follow.

A CODE grant has become a powerful signal to other donors and employers that the charity in question is doing many things well. Endowment funding, says one grantee, gave his group credibility "to raise additional major philanthropic investments and…to approach potential employer clients." Peer funders also benefit from CODE's clear, even-handed process. They look to CODE for recommendations because they can trust its audits of baseline operations and results among its grantees. By making its processes public and transparent, CODE is making the allocation of donor dollars a much more efficient process. And more donations are ending up at organizations with the capability to provide good outcomes.

Finally, the endowment uses its visibility and public following (and that of the parent company) to support grantees and draw constructive attention to the issue of employing veterans. This has boosted many groups and useful undertakings.

Recruiting partners
CODE has distributed over $16 million to nonprofits providing job services to vets, and has another $6 million in grants planned for 2017. CODE's parent company covers all of the administrative costs and overhead of the charity, including the director's salary, so all endowment spending goes to direct grants. In addition to the funding that Activision Blizzard has put into the endowment, the company encourages Goldenberg and the board to fundraise directly to the public (through special company products that make it easy for consumers to give) and to other corporate donors (through company partnerships). Structuring CODE as a separate nonprofit, rather than a corporate foundation, allows it to take in funding from these outside sources. And it lets givers who want to help vets but don't have the expertise that has been created at CODE to give with great effectiveness. Much of the growth in CODE's grantmaking budget is now coming from these external donations—$3 million in 2016.

Because of the rigor with which it evaluates organizations, and its businesslike approach to giving, the endowment has been able to engineer partnerships with a variety of companies that trust its grants. These include Costco, Carl's/Hardees, Redbox, Gamestop, and Amazon. In 2015 alone, these partner companies raised $1.4 million for CODE.

Activision Blizzard also allows CODE access to its customers. Call of Duty buyers assume the identities of warriors in their game playing, and many are naturally inclined to support real veterans. Goldenberg has been able to launch several products that funnel small donations to CODE, including in-game "personalization packs" that have raised more than $600,000, a five-day gaming marathon streamed to millions of viewers that raised more than $200,000, and a campaign where users could bid to become actors in a new Call of Duty game. Ancillary products like "Call of Duty dogtags" are also now sold to generate revenue for the charity. It's worth noting that one thing the endowment has never done to raise money is to cash in on the inaccurate portrayal of veterans as hapless and pitiful victims, as some charities have tried.

Overall, the Call of Duty Endowment has been a striking success. Hard numbers testify to that. So far, CODE funding has put more than 25,000 veterans to work. Over the latest two years, the organization reduced the average cost of placing each veteran in a job by 54 percent—to under $600 per individual. At the same time, the quality of the jobs acquired went up. Last year, the average starting salary of veterans who were placed in work by a CODE-funded organization increased 18 percent, to $50,364. Not bad for an organization that began with some disappointing grants.

Brewing Up Jobs:
Starbucks's Howard Schultz helps veterans and employers sit down together

Gallon for gallon, early morning by late night, servicemembers drink as much coffee as any other segment of the U.S. population. But there's more than a love of java connecting veterans and Starbucks. The company's chairman, Howard Schultz, has committed $30 million, many hours, and a chunk of his fame as a modern business icon to help open up opportunities for veterans in America. In particular, his Schultz Family Foundation aims to smooth the transition from military to civilian work by providing newly minted veterans with career training in high-demand fields.

Schultz is a paragon of American economic mobility. He grew up in public housing in Brooklyn, then attended Northern Michigan University on an athletic scholarship, becoming the first in his family to go to college. After a series of sales jobs, he convinced the founders of a fledgling coffee company called Starbucks to hire him. Having expanded the little operation into a global behemoth, Schultz is now a billionaire and one of the most recognizable business leaders in the world.

With his wife Sheri, Howard established the Schultz Family Foundation to give other Americans access to opportunities for success regardless of their background. As foundation director Daniel Pitasky puts it, "our work is really about closing the divide that prevents folks from realizing their potential." The foundation focuses on two initiatives. Onward Youth seeks to help the 5.6 million young people ages 16 to 24 who are neither working nor in school by pulling them into training programs that lead to jobs. Onward Veterans supports post-9/11 veterans and their families as they transition to civilian life.

Schultz learned that soldiers were more concerned by the prospect of finding a job once they left the military than they were about deploying overseas.

Like most Americans, Schultz has always appreciated the military—his father was a World War II veteran. But it was a 2011 visit to West Point to speak at a leadership forum that set him on his current path. He met with several cadets and military faculty members before his talk, hearing about their lives and experiences in the armed forces. He came away feeling he had more to learn from them than they did from him. That personal moment stuck with him.

In 2012, former Defense Secretary Robert Gates joined the Starbucks board of directors. He and Schultz began to talk regularly about this generation of veterans. They arranged for Medal of Honor winner Leroy Petry to speak to Starbucks employees in Seattle. Again Schultz was struck by the humility and quiet competence of the soldier.

At that point Schultz decided to act. He wanted to do his part, but had to figure out what that should be. He didn't outsource learning about the topic—Howard and Sheri started visiting military bases in the U.S. from which servicemembers were deploying, medical centers in which the injured were recovering, and even a U.S. military base in Kuwait. At Joint Base Lewis McChord, just 20 miles from his home in Seattle, Schultz heard something from the command sergeant major that surprised him: Many soldiers were more concerned by the prospect of finding a job once they left the military than they were about deploying overseas. Putting people to work in the private sector? That was a topic Schultz, having built a company with 238,000 employees, knew something about.

Diagnosing, educating, partnering

"Most of us try to set up our next job before we leave our current job," notes the Schultz Foundation's Pitasky. "It should be no different for transitioning servicemembers." But for many veterans, that doesn't happen. In 2012, the last year for which this data has been released, 49 percent of all separating servicemembers ended up on unemployment compensation.

One of the first things that Pitasky discovered is that servicemembers often didn't start preparing for their civilian career until they were just a few months away from leaving the military. The government programs intended to help with the military-to-civilian transition were inadequate. There was an obvious disconnect between the focus of current veteran training programs and what employers were actually looking for. "It was clear that there wasn't engagement with the private sector."

And on the private-sector side, "more and more companies were realizing the value of hiring veterans and military spouses but they told us they were having trouble finding and engaging them." In short, vets didn't know how to find jobs, and employers didn't know how to find qualified vets. Schultz was in a position to do something about these things. In 2014, after completing their initial research, Howard and Sheri launched the Onward Veterans initiative with an initial donation of $30 million.

Schultz believes that transition is made harder by the fact that military personnel and civilians have so little understanding of one another. "I don't think we've ever lived through a situation where the American people have been so disconnected from the military, their families, and the unbelievable sacrifice they have pursued on our behalf," he said a few years ago. "The question for all of us now is how do we bridge the divide between the military and civilians? That is the challenge of the day."

As part of his personal effort to raise awareness of the contributions servicemembers make to the nation, not just in uniform, but also after they transition out, Schultz partnered with *Washington Post* reporter Rajiv Chandrasekaran to produce a 2014 book of stories from veterans Schultz had met during his learning tour. In *For Love of Country,* Schultz and Chandrasekaran mix tales of distinguished service in battle with descriptions of contributions made by veterans at home. The book sold well, with all proceeds funneled to charities supporting veterans and military families.

That same year, Schultz formed a partnership with HBO and JPMorgan Chase to host a Veterans' Day concert on the National Mall that mixed performances from artists like Bruce Springsteen with stories of veterans profiled in *For Love of Country*. This too was an effort to bridge the civilian-military divide, by describing real acts of servicemembers and veterans to the wider public.

Soon after announcing his $30 million commitment, Schultz and his foundation began looking for organizational partners. In particular, says Pitasky, they were looking for collaborators who were "'trilingual'— able to work with the veterans service community, the Department of Defense, and the corporate sector." Syracuse University's Institute for Veterans and Military Families (see Case Study Three in *Serving Those Who Served*) became an important ally. Since its founding in 2011 IVMF has quickly become a national leader in research and job- and business-related programming for vets. IVMF managing director Jim McDonough worked closely with the Schultz Foundation to build employment pipelines for veterans.

Employers generally value broad military competencies like leadership, work ethic, and teamwork. But for many of their new hires, employers need specific proficiencies in IT, customer service, medical technology, project management, and such, skills that many veterans need to be trained in before starting civilian jobs. "We had to offer candidates technical competencies that matched their strong soft skills to really advantage them in the eyes of private employers," says McDonough. "Then we're in a position to ask our private-sector partners to guarantee interviews." The goal was to build a path that presented hiring managers with very qualified candidates with few barriers to entry. After that, "it's up to the veteran to win the job."

Working with the Defense Department

The plan put together by the Schultz Foundation depended on preparing servicemembers before they transitioned out of service. To make that work, cooperation was needed from the Department of Defense. Many donors struggle mightily with government bureaucracies. Under certain circumstances, however, joint efforts can work. Schultz has had some success with the collaboration it calls Onward to Opportunity, or O2O.

The O2O team signed a memorandum of understanding with the Defense Department that blessed Schultz's efforts to offer members of the military civilian job training including apprenticeships and internships before they separate from the military, under three constraints: Servicemembers had to be within six months of separation, the training offered had to lead to a high probability of employment, and the servicemember had to have approval from his or her commander.

> Working with the Defense Department has required many bureaucratic twists and turns. Even an agreement with the Secretary of Defense only cuts so deep.

While they viewed this agreement as a major accomplishment, the Schultz Family Foundation and its helpers at IVMF would soon discover that every individual base commander could interpret the agreement differently and control the way it was implemented on his or her base. Local commanders were justifiably concerned that too much focus on post-military careers could distract from a unit's military readiness. O2O ended up requiring heavy base-by-base negotiation.

The base that ended up being most helpful was just 20 miles from Starbucks headquarters: Joint Base Lewis-McChord. A pilot program launched there in 2015 with a small cohort of participants. Success begat success, and when the program showed solid results at Lewis-McChord, there was a willingness to launch it at Camp Pendleton in San Diego. With each new base opening, the next base becomes more amenable. The process, however, has required many bureaucratic twists and turns. An agreement with the Secretary of Defense only cuts so deep.

How O2O Works

The Schultz Family Foundation funded IVMF to administer the resulting programs. Not only Defense officials and individual base officers but also local employers and training organizations had to be juggled. At each base, two IVMF staff members set up shop in the office charged with coordinating servicemember transitions to civilian life. These staffers market the Onward to Opportunity program, recruit participants (both military and spouses), and deliver training content. They also arrange for local employers to come in to add an extra degree of reality to the training.

Once commanders clear them to participate, servicemembers attend an orientation where the program's expectations and opportunities are spelled out. Then participants complete a detailed assessment of their abilities. IVMF's centralized enrollment team reviews these and, with some one-on-one counseling, helps each participant find a broad industry track (like IT or customer service) and specific skill credential (like Cisco Certified Network Technician) that could match him or her to a job.

The training courses take place online, supplemented with in-person content from local trainers and businesses. They usually take around 13 weeks to complete. At first, these pathways were produced by IVMF with industry input. But as the program matured, employers and training specialists were invited to provide portions of the training.

About a third of the way through the training regimen, O2O connects participants with Hire Heroes USA and Corporate America Supports You, two excellent nonprofits that specialize in coaching veterans through the job search process. They talk about goals and career plans and logistics. If it becomes apparent that a current training path is not a good match, they help the candidate switch. At the 80 percent completion mark, HHUSA and CASY start matching candidates with specific job opportunities at employers in the O2O database (after less than a year of operation, there are already 274 of them). The groups help candidates prepare for actual job applications.

Around 50 percent of those who take the initial O2O career assessment also complete the recommended skill training (though that rate is decreasing as more tracks are added). O2O doesn't necessarily see attrition as negative—finding out what you don't like or can't master is valuable too. The goal is to help servicemembers make informed decisions about their future careers. Sometimes that involves a false start and redirection.

IVMF teams (with some help from Howard Schultz himself) have recruited companies of all sizes to O2O—like Amazon, WellMed, and Starbucks.

Local employers in the vicinity of individual bases have also been drawn in. As this employer pool grows and changes, IVMF, HHUSA, and CASY adjust their training and coaching of participants to match the skills participating employers need. When they complete their training, participants receive an industry-recognized certification and a guaranteed interview with a partner employer. They still have to earn a job, but about 80 percent of O2O graduates get hired by partner companies.

By the end of 2016, the program was up and running at nine military bases, and providing services to servicemembers and spouses from 40 smaller bases in the same region. The program currently offers four broad job tracks and 20 training pathways. Expansion will continue. On O2O's first base, a third of transitioning vets were approved to participate, and one quarter of those went through the program. So far, about two thirds of the participants have been servicemembers, and one third spouses.

The ultimate goal is to run four to six training cohorts of 75 participants, every year, at 18 bases. That would involve placing around 4,500 trained veterans annually in good careers. Another 3,500 will go right into the job market with O2O support limited to job search, interview skills, and résumé preparation. The program will cost around $11 million to run per year. In 2013, the Defense Department's unemployment compensation bill alone topped $825 million. If O2O reduces dependence on unemployment by just 2 percent, it will save the government more than it costs Schultz. On the private-sector side, new hires typically cost employers around $4,000; O2O costs $1,600 per up-skilled placement and about $500 for direct hires. And it costs veterans nothing.

Vets in Tech: Marc & Laura Andreessen make connections

Laura Arrillaga-Andreessen has philanthropic roots and shoots all around her. She is a director of the Arrillaga Foundation established by her father John Arrillaga, who developed much of Silicon Valley's real estate into headquarters for leading computer firms. She and her husband, tech entrepreneur and venture capitalist Marc Andreessen, created a joint foundation. Laura also runs her own foundation with a particular focus on helping donors become better informed. And she teaches classes about philanthropy at Stanford business school.

The Andreessens have always been interested in "protecting our protectors," says Simon Shachter, program manager at the Laura Arrillaga-Andreessen Foundation, and they've given substantially to support local police forces, CIA and FBI officers, and veterans. The couple also have an interest in strengthening the talent pipeline that feeds technology companies. Recently they noticed that veterans are sharply underrepresented in tech-industry jobs in Silicon Valley, and began to tie these two threads together.

Learning about the field took some work. "None of us were military ourselves, or knew that experience very well. And there wasn't much information publicly available." They started gathering background from the few other donors and organizations that had shown an interest in including veterans in technology jobs. These included the Call of Duty Endowment and Stanford University. Connections through Marc's venture-capital firm—Andreessen Horowitz—were also helpful.

With each new contact they would "first ask about their personal experience." Hearing individual stories was helpful, whether it involved learning what veterans were dealing with, what companies were facing, or how nonprofits were helping. The question they aimed to answer, says Shachter, was "why is tech a place where veterans seem to be underrepresented, and how can we change that?"

When they announced their new Veteran Inclusion Grants in a blog post, the Andreessens explained what this research had told them, and what their mission would be as a result. Veterans, they found, had many of the qualities tech employers sorely need. But they lack "resources and networks with which to channel their incredible life experiences and training into productive opportunities." Andreessen grantmaking would try to address those deficiencies "to help veterans, their families, and the companies they work for achieve their full potential."

The foundation went looking for nonprofits "where a small infusion of cash now can produce maximum impact later." Shachter and his colleagues sought promising organizations that could be "launched into another phase. We wanted to help prove their models, and get them on the radars of larger funders." The Andreessens would make grants to build organizational capacity—"help nonprofits strengthen their infrastructure and run more effectively and efficiently."

They also wanted groups capable of measuring the effects of their work. "Laura teaches all the time that evaluation has to be baked into everything you do as a nonprofit. So we ask nonprofits how are they going to evaluate the programs they want us to fund, and what extra money they might need for that."

The LAAF team whittled down the pool of potential grant recipients and eventually settled on four charities: The COMMIT Foundation, VetsinTech, the Institute for Veterans and Military Families, and the Honor Foundation. These, the Andreessens wrote in their announcement, are tackling the issue of veteran inclusion "from four unique perspectives," with "innovative programs and interventions."

The grant to the COMMIT Foundation allowed that group to hire a new employee to work with tech corporations like Facebook hoping to hire veterans. The foundation will educate companies on the special skills and capacities of vets, and help job applicants connect with hiring managers and then succeed occupationally once they are employed. The Andreessens likewise funded additional staff for VetsinTech. This will expand their programs for training and placing new veterans in tech careers.

At the Institute for Veterans and Military Families run by Syracuse University, one of the largest and longest running organizations devoted to boosting veterans into entrepreneurship and employment, the Andreessen grant created "an alumni network to connect graduates of the seven programs they run." And at the Honor Foundation, which assists

Special Operations vets as they shift to civilian careers, the Andreessens paid for computer equipment that will improve the group's online-learning programs, and give them new abilities to measure and analyze the effectiveness of their offerings.

All of these nonprofits featured "compelling leaders, and were just beginning to establish a track record," summed up Shachter. So "we were able to step in early and push them to the next level."
—*Troy White*

Emphasizing Education:
Jerome Kohlberg connects veterans to campuses

Since 2009, the Post-9/11 G.I. Bill has helped over 1.2 million vets pursue higher education. Given the solid connection between advanced education and increased lifetime earnings, it's safe to say that this program has been one of the most productive veterans' benefits since the original G.I. Bill was enacted back in 1944. Unsurprisingly, philanthropy, and one committed donor in particular, had a strategic role in re-launching the G.I. Bill for the current era. His generosity is also playing a key role in helping to improve successful use of the benefit.

Jerome Kohlberg, known as "Mr. K" to many of those who knew him, served in the Navy during World War II and then used the original G.I. Bill to get a great education. He was always grateful for the help in getting ahead in life. "I was 17 when I signed up in the Navy. Then I went to Swarthmore, Harvard Business School, and law school at Columbia, all on the G.I. Bill. And we got a stipend to live on!" After his service and schooling, Kohlberg went to work on Wall Street, and became a spectacularly successful investor. He co-founded one of the original private equity firms, Kohlberg Kravis Roberts, and has been hailed as the "spiritual father of the entire leveraged buyout business."

Before his death in 2015, Kohlberg was a wide-ranging and active donor for decades. Despite his generosity and influence in philanthropy for veterans, he was a very quiet giver. He shared a belief with Ronald Reagan that "there is no limit to what a man can do or where he can go if he doesn't mind who gets the credit."

Spotting a problem

Kohlberg's impact on veterans' philanthropy began somewhat accidentally. In 2002, he hired a Marine Reservist named Matthew Boulay to manage his scholarship program at Swarthmore. (In line with his quiet giving style, Mr. K named that effort after his college roommate.) Only six months after Matthew was hired, his unit was called to active duty and deployed to Iraq. Rather than being annoyed by this disruption, Kohlberg was extremely supportive. He told Matthew, for instance, that "everyone in the office was on call to help his wife, 24/7. 'If she needs anything anytime, I'll give the order that everyone can drop what they're doing and help her out even if it's in the middle of the workday.'"

A few years later, in 2006, Matthew was back from war, still working for Mr. K and getting his master's degree. During an incidental conversation, the topic of what G.I. Bill benefits Matthew was using to pay for his degree came up. Kohlberg was doubly shocked—first at the exorbitant cost of higher education, and second at how small the G.I. Bill stipends had become.

The first G.I. Bill provided veterans with payments large enough to completely cover the cost of most educational programs. The benefit was updated after the Korean and Vietnam wars, and again in 1984, becoming the Montgomery G.I. Bill. Over time, though, the value of the benefit ebbed so that, by 1990, it was worth (in constant dollars) only one third of its 1945 value. At the same time, the cost of higher education had risen dramatically.

Scholarships and advocacy

Kohlberg initiated a two-pronged response to his discovery. It coupled direct philanthropy to address higher-education shortfalls immediately with advocacy aimed at changing policy for the long term. This included full-need scholarships funded by his donations and allies he recruited, along with a publicity campaign to document inadequacies in the existing Montgomery G.I. Bill. Kohlberg also put his own time and energy into reaching out personally to policymakers to advocate an update of the educational benefit for former soldiers, sailors, marines, and airmen.

Mr. K commissioned Scholarship America, a national nonprofit that specializes in managing academic awards for students, to run the scholarship portion of his initiative. The organization mostly manages corporate scholarships that are made available to children of employees, but its leadership included retired military officers, and its chairman had led a special campaign to provide scholarships for the children of 9/11 victims, so Scholarship America jumped at the opportunity to execute Kohlberg's vision. The group took responsibility for developing applications, advertising to eligible candidates, reviewing submissions, and selecting recipients. It also worked with schools to complete paperwork necessary to execute the scholarships.

These awards covered students pursuing four-year programs, associate degrees, and vocational certificates. They covered students who were veterans, active duty, Reservists, and National Guardsmen. And efforts were made to provide grants in every state, across rural and urban areas.

Kohlberg funded these scholarships through his giving vehicles, the Kohlberg Foundation and the Kisco Foundation, on a full-need basis— covering any financial shortfall students faced after all other sources of funding (G.I. Bill, school financial aid, other scholarships) had been tapped. Boulay, who worked side-by-side with Mr. K throughout this effort, explains that it was the donor's intention to stick with recipients through graduation, no matter what delays or disruptions they might face due to deployment or needs to work or be with family.

The scholarship was deliberately low-barrier—it didn't require any minimum GPA or performance checks beyond whatever requirements the schools set. Beginning in 2007, Scholarship America enrolled new recipients every semester on a first-come, first-served basis, eventually supporting around 500 veterans. Mr. K put more than $8 million into this effort, and he had an even bigger plan.

A new G.I. Bill

Kohlberg recognized that ultimately there needed to be a new G.I. Bill for this new generation of veterans. So while he was personally aiding a wide variety of individuals, he was also using his program to raise awareness. Each of his recipients became a walking, talking demonstration of the value of investing in higher education of those leaving service.

"It was a way of telling the story of veterans and education. If people asked 'why are you giving veterans scholarships when we have a G.I. Bill?'," Boulay points out, "we could have that conversation." A core tenet of Mr. K's approach to advocacy was elevating the voices of individuals affected by policies and problems so they could speak for themselves. This echoed throughout his philanthropic efforts for veterans. "He would just fly in veterans from Iowa to tell their story, which they would otherwise never have a chance to lay out. That seemed like the right way to make policy," says Boulay.

> Kohlberg put his own time and energy into reaching out to policymakers to advocate for an update of the educational benefit.

At the same time, they began supporting and linking a coalition of veterans' organizations interested in the idea of a new G.I. Bill. Kohlberg funded newer organizations like Student Veterans of America and Iraq and Afghanistan Veterans of America that worked alongside older groups like Vietnam Veterans of America and the Military Officers Association of America. Meanwhile Kohlberg met personally with various members of Congress to make the case for a new G.I. Bill. He didn't push his own version of what an expanded G.I. Bill would look like, and didn't see "tinkering with the policy process as our role or our goal," explains Boulay. He just "wanted to provide some momentum as an outside champion."

Eventually Senator James Webb presented a bill that seemed to match Kohlberg's general goals. He said later in a newspaper interview, "I visited with three or four senators, all of whom had used the original G.I. Bill the same as myself." He also noted that "the military was against it because they felt it would hurt re-enlistment."

Kohlberg's foundation put together an event at City College of New York, Colin Powell's alma mater, and Mr. K invited Powell, who until then had been skeptical about the costs of a new G.I. Bill, to attend. Powell ultimately gave a speech in support of expanding educational benefits for veterans, and "within two weeks we had 76 senators and got the thing done," as Kohlberg puts it. The Post-9/11 G.I. Bill was signed into law by President Bush in 2008. It included 36 months of full funding for tuition at any public university (or the equivalent at a private school), plus a stipend for housing and books.

Helping community colleges connect to vets

The Kohlberg team also realized that community colleges play a vital role for vets. During the 2011-2012 school year, 37 percent of all student veterans who used the G.I. Bill went to community college to be trained for jobs like nurse or electrician. In 2015 they created the Kohlberg Prize to encourage community colleges to serve veterans even better. It provided an $80,000 grant that allowed recipient institutions to plan how they could improve student services to veterans. When their plan was approved, they received a second grant of $100,000 to implement the initiative.

About $1 million in Kohlberg Prize grants were distributed. Says Boulay, "what's exciting is the range of schools, some urban, some rural— there's an agricultural program at one; there's this high-tech cybersecurity program at another. Community colleges vary wonderfully in terms of the programs they offer and the specialties they have." The schools cover the country from Salem, Oregon, to Baltimore, Maryland.

As part of the process, schools were required to document their expansion and share what they learned with other colleges. The recipients thus became exemplars and models for many other peer institutions. "We didn't have to find the ten very best schools in the country. The purpose here is to lift some up and have learning come out of this, which we then share and spread around." Jerome Kohlberg, explains Boulay, "didn't want credit, but he wanted his giving to set an example."

Recruit, Retain, and Educate: Bill Ahmanson encourages colleges to remember vets

In Southern California, you can't throw a stone among the core cultural and educational institutions without hitting something the Ahmanson Foundation has supported. It was an early funder of the Los Angeles County Museum of Art, the Ahmanson Theater, the California Museum of Science and Industry, the Ahmanson Center for Biological Research, Ahmanson Technology Center, Ahmanson-Getty Fellowship, and the Ahmanson Foundation Humanities Endowment

Fund, among others, which dot the landscape of higher education in the region. In addition, it has given substantially to medicine and health services, preservation of the environment, ending homelessness, and supporting low-income populations. Broadly, its mission is to "increase the quality of life in Southern California and to enhance its cultural legacy."To say that the foundation of the late financier Howard Ahmanson and his nephews Robert and William is a bedrock Los Angeles institution is an understatement.

Around 2010, foundation president Bill Ahmanson, William's son, noticed an uptick in the number of young veterans returning to the L.A. area from Iraq and Afghanistan. He decided the foundation should help make sure those transitions were smooth. He received plenty of proposals mentioning veterans, but few were targeted tightly on vets—"they were just tossing in the name 'veterans' to get people like us to loosen up the purse strings."

> I got everything from a chilly "let me check with admissions" to "we were just talking about this— are you involved in corporate espionage?"

Veterans had become the cause of the day, a fundraising tool of choice, but despite the public discussion not much was happening in programming. At the V.A. there were lots of ideas "but nothing was gelling," according to Ahmanson, and "I got tired of all the handwringing and people wondering 'What are we going to do?' So we did something on our own."

Foundation leaders asked themselves, "what can we do specifically for veterans in a space where we're already comfortable? We did some research and learned about the Yellow Ribbon program at the Philanthropy Roundtable meeting in October 2012." By then the Post-9/11 G.I. Bill was up and running and had nearly 650,000 users. So was Yellow Ribbon, a V.A. program that matches dollar for dollar any funding universities put up to cover attendance costs that exceed what the G.I. Bill provides. It is mostly used by expensive private schools.

Building on familiar ground
Higher education was something the Ahmanson Foundation knew well, and where it was confident it could find opportunities to make

a difference. Bill sensed that "80 to 90 percent of today's new veterans are basically squared away and need just some direction and education." Some veterans, though, were struggling to complete their degrees. Some weren't going to the right schools for their needs. Some of those attending private colleges (where fees sometimes exceed even the generous payments of the new G.I. Bill) were graduating with lots of debt. There were issues of adjustment and culture and support that could make the college experiences of vets especially successful if they were addressed.

So the program that emerged—the Ahmanson Veteran Scholarship Initiative—isn't directed at tuition or student living costs. Instead, the AVSI makes annual $50,000 grants to colleges (for seven to ten years) to help them "recruit, retain, and educate veterans." Before making this commitment Bill called two college presidents to test the idea. Then he took it to his board for a vote. The effort was conceived and approved in record time.

Ahmanson then made a series of calls to heads of colleges and universities that went something like this: "'I want to see if you would accept a grant to create new procedures on your campus to recruit, educate, and retain veterans all the way to graduation. My board has already approved it.' This would usually be followed by dead silence on the other end of the phone. Then I got everything from a chilly 'let me check with admissions to see if we need it' to 'we were just talking about this the other day—are you involved in some corporate espionage?'"

After four years, the basic structure of AVSI remains roughly the same as when it launched. About two dozen colleges are participating. All of them are private, four-year undergraduate schools in California, but that's about all they have in common. They include some science and engineering schools, business schools, women's colleges, three art schools, and a myriad of liberal-arts colleges—places like the University of Southern California, Art Center College of Design, and Pomona College.

Bill explains that these schools are good partners for the Ahmanson Foundation. The foundation has worked with most of them for decades, and knows their leadership, the quality of their education, and the ways they operate. Because they're all private institutions where tuition is usually higher than what the G.I. Bill will pay, they are likely to have students facing the kinds of challenges the foundation wants to tackle. And making these high-level private schools better fits for veterans is a valuable public service—because "just like for anybody else, large public institutions are not always the best fit for a veteran," and Bill wanted to increase individual educational choices for former servicemembers.

Programming evolves as colleges learn

One major goal for the Ahmanson Foundation was to increase the total number of veterans at each participating college. A few of them had substantial veteran populations before AVSI began, but most did not. That's an imbalance many other elite private universities share—Harvard, MIT, Princeton, Duke, and many other top institutions all have fewer than five veterans on their campuses as undergraduates.

It isn't that vets don't qualify to get into these schools; there are significant numbers of students just out of the military doing superbly at top schools like Columbia, Georgetown, University of Southern California, and Syracuse. But many elite colleges have no idea how to advertise to veterans, inform them of their opportunities, or make the small adjustments in application processes or enrollment processes needed by students who don't follow the conventional "right out of high school" path to campus.

Bill Ahmanson started small by challenging the colleges participating in his initiative to take the One More Vet Pledge—promising to enroll at least one more veteran every year than they had the year prior. AVSI also helped schools invest in college fairs for veterans, marketing to veterans, and tasking college counselors to do outreach and help veterans through the application process. A couple of institutions set up partnerships with American Honors, a program that identifies talented veterans enrolled in community colleges across the country who are looking to transfer to four-year institutions. Within two years, many schools "blew the doors off" their Pledge commitments. Some schools reached triple-digit numbers of veteran undergrads.

As they learned how to get vets on campus, administrators shifted their focus to new challenges they never anticipated, like crediting veterans for relevant advanced training and experience they received in the military. Most colleges have viewed military training as too foreign to map onto college transcripts. The foundation encouraged AVSI schools to reconsider. Not allowing veterans credit for skills they've already acquired is a waste of school resources, veterans' time, and G.I. Bill money, they noted.

"When you've got somebody whose job it was to monitor Arabic communications chatter and then direct troops, they can pass three semesters of Arabic. These aren't weak credits—the military refresher course for Arabic is a thousand hours. The military certificate in higher mathematics for an engineer on a nuclear submarine means something," states Ahmanson. "Schools were hesitant to do it initially, but they ended up figuring it out. They had to do a lot of that translation on their own." Occidental College stands out as one early adopter that saw the value of offering credit for military experience and helped lead the pack.

AVSI schools have also shifted some of their funding to allow veterans to graduate with less debt. The V.A.'s Yellow Ribbon program matches resources schools put up from their own funds to fill the gap between private tuitions and reimbursements allowed under the G.I. Bill. In many cases, Ahmanson funding opens up new Yellow Ribbon spots at these private schools.

> Many elite colleges have no idea how to advertise to veterans. It isn't that vets don't qualify to get into these schools.

Trust and latitude yield programs that last

The Ahmanson Foundation intentionally set up its initiative with loose instructions. "We ask them to report back, 'what are you doing to recruit? What are you doing to retain? What are you doing to educate?'" says Ahmanson. So "we can see what they're doing, but we give them maximum latitude. Some things they do may not seem important to us, but may be important to their campus culture."

Every college is different, and letting them find their own ways of succeeding will ultimately result in better service to veterans, Ahmanson believes. He sets the finish line and lets each school experiment with how to get there. The foundation's only non-negotiable requirement is that schools not coddle veterans. "A lot of veteran centers I find are all about making excuses and babysitting. That's not what we do."

One important way the foundation has encouraged high standards and energetic experimentation to discover the best solutions for vets is by making a comparatively long commitment to the joint effort. The seven- to ten-year AVSI grant periods are an eternity compared to the one-year "funding whipsaw" it usually gets from government funding.

"Initially, they were pretty tight-fisted with the money because they didn't know how long it was going to last. Now that we're going into our fourth year, they're starting to realize this has some longevity to it. They're being more creative with it, and they know this is a population they'll be able to continue to serve."

The Ahmanson Foundation's long-term goal is to make veterans a normal part of campus culture, so that when specialized funding eventually winds down, the schools will have a steady, normal stream of former military members. By investing in helping them learn how to serve student veterans, the foundation is helping colleges discover the intrinsic value of having them on campus. Because the grantees are allowed the flexibility to decide how to spend the money toward AVSI's goals, they're more likely to add their own resources and keep the program going after AVSI closes down.

Ahmanson explains that "this is where I think philanthropy is most helpful. We help identify important priorities. But we let them frame the response for themselves, without a lot of strings and restrictions, so they can make it their own priority. And they all have."

After four years and $5 million of funding, the signals are very positive. A total of 25 potent private schools have significantly increased the number of veterans on their campuses. They have overcome barriers that made recruitment difficult and prior credit rare. And they have kept enrolled all the way to graduation many individuals who would likely have dropped out. Some schools have even launched additional fundraising and made six-figure commitments to complement their $50,000 annual gift from the Ahmanson Foundation.

One more non-traditional gift for non-traditional students

The Ahmanson Foundation's most recent project supporting student veterans is a departure from the rest of its AVSI funding. Fully half of all veterans have families when they go back to school. This makes them completely different from most other undergraduates. And in most cases the housing allowances included in the G.I. Bill housing are not enough to fully cover the exorbitant rents of Southern California.

When Bill Ahmanson became aware that a set of family apartment units near the Occidental College campus was going up for sale, he made the school a proposal. The foundation would buy the building, then proffer specifically to house the families of students who are former servicemembers. Any units not occupied by Occidental students would be made available to other families of veterans attending AVSI colleges in that part of Los Angeles. And Occidental would only charge rents in the amount of the G.I. Bill housing allowance.

Occidental agreed. The college even offered to open certain other campus facilities to the families residing in the building. The Ahmanson Foundation put up $7 million to purchase the building.

Bringing in the National Champions:
The Albertson Foundation aids rural veterans

The J. A. and Kathryn Albertson Foundation stands out from the other philanthropies in this guidebook in that it's fully focused on Idaho, a predominantly rural state that ranks 39th in the U.S. by population. Idaho is a less expensive location for most kinds of programming. And its size and lack of bureaucracy make it possible to create high-impact, state-wide programs relatively quickly. The flip side is that low population density can make it hard to maintain offices and staffing in convenient locations across the state, and challenging to find or home-grow nonprofit service providers that can carry out specialized work.

Since it was established in 1966 from the fortune of grocer Joe Albertson and his wife, the Albertson Foundation has invested $700 million in promoting education and "limitless learning for all Idahoans." Under the current leadership of Jamie Jo Scott, Albertson's great granddaughter, the foundation doesn't just cut checks to organizations and ideas it likes. It often incubates campaigns in-house before spinning them off into separate organizations.

Many prior initiatives have focused on improving K-12 education, like bringing Teach For America to the state, and developing "Don't Fail Idaho," an awareness campaign to make education reform a top local priority. "We view the investments we make," says Scott, "as a vehicle to a better economic outcome for Idaho's future." Oftentimes, "that involves recruiting talent, and keeping it here. With homegrown talent we want to make sure they have opportunities, and don't have to leave to take advantage of them. To new talent we want to send a message: 'You're a leader, you're a student, you're an entrepreneur—we want you.' It's trying to sell the state we believe in."

A new effort to serve veterans

In 2013, the foundation started looking at places beyond education where it could have these effects. There was a willingness to consider cultivating veterans as a source of talent in Idaho. The board invited me, as The Philanthropy Roundtable's program director on veterans, to speak at one of the meetings. I encouraged the foundation to treat veterans as civic assets, not damaged goods.

This resonated, because, as Scott put it, "we have a bit of a leadership drought in Idaho." The idea of cultivating veterans as local leaders appealed to Blossom Johnston, the program officer at the foundation who had overseen many of its education projects. "In some of our rural communities, for instance, we have problems getting good school board members. It's a lot of work and a very thankless job. But with the right people, we could see the education system turn around in a big way." The foundation also envisioned veterans helping to transform communities through their work in businesses and government. "We want veterans or their spouses on city councils, chambers of commerce, the state legislature," Johnston notes, "or in the governor's office."

Despite its enthusiasm for cultivating veterans as state leaders, the foundation had not found any local organization around which it could build much momentum. Then Scott and Johnston attended a talk at a 2014 Philanthropy Roundtable meeting featuring two founders of stellar national organizations for vets. Eric Greitens is founder of The Mission Continues, a group that encourages and enables civilian service by former members of the military. Jake Wood is co-founder of Team Rubicon, which organizes veterans to offer volunteer assistance to communities after disasters hit. Inspired by their presentations, Scott and Johnston saw these groups as the kinds of organizations they could build statewide efforts from. So they committed the foundation and began to map out an approach.

Johnston's mandate was to do the most she could for the largest number of Idahoans. In practical terms this meant the foundation would not consider high-cost, long-horizon programs like health care or mental-health treatment. An Idaho veteran and businessman advising her, Joe Forney, warned that issues like mental health could become a "black hole," with a high risk of entangling the foundation with problems endemic to the dysfunctional V.A. bureaucracy. Three focus groups of Idaho veterans commissioned by Johnston urged the foundation to focus on important practical aspects of the transition from military to civilian life, like jobs and community involvement.

Recruiting the nation's best

On the surface, it seemed like there were lots of veterans' organizations in Idaho. But looks were deceiving. Many of the existing groups fell prey to the "veterans as victims" approach, or didn't meet the foundation's emphasis on building up people and organizations into self-sufficiency, or lacked the strong leadership needed to expand. This left two options: build up groups from scratch, or find national nonprofits that were doing great work and convince them to come to Idaho. For Johnston, the choice was obvious. Convincing successful charities to expand to Idaho would be less difficult and less risky. So her team began looking for the very best nonprofits for veterans in the country.

Albertson spent about a year vetting different organizations, getting to know their leadership, culture, operating procedures, and measures of success. Scott identifies four major themes that run through all of the organizations the foundation eventually invited to Idaho:

"First, they don't see veterans as victims, and they try to target a population of veterans who truly want to be helped. They don't see themselves as enabling vehicles; they see themselves as leading to self-betterment. They talk about themselves differently, they attract a population that is not interested in being dependent."

"Second, they operate with a true sense of being really good at one thing, or maybe two things. They have mastered the work they care about, and don't try to do everything. Some organizations that tackle complex issues flounder into doing hundreds of things, none of them well. It's easy to fall prey to mission creep."

"Third, the groups we chose make important changes in the way they operate based on what they see is and isn't working. They have business acumen, carefully measure their effects, and care about the impact they're having."

"Last, these groups have built incredible leadership teams. Leadership is the key to everything else."

> You can have big, unambiguous effects in rural areas. We have so much less scar tissue and sclerosis and bureaucratic inertia.

Once it had identified the most promising partners, Albertson faced the challenge of convincing each group to expand to a place it had not previously considered. Scott and the team were undaunted. "We do this all the time," because Idaho is not on many must-include lists. "It's easy for us, because we love our state," and it has discovered that the more people learn about it, the likelier they are to be impressed.

Their pitch as evangelists for Idaho went something like this: You can have big, unambiguous effects here. We recruited Teach For America here under the same premise, and it proved out. We have so much less scar tissue and sclerosis and bureaucratic inertia—you can come here, work for a year, and transform a community. When you go to bigger states and cities there are often a variety of services that already exist. We have nothing like your services here, and there is a hungry audience. We've done this with education-reform groups, we've done this with venture-capital groups. You will see clear successes.

Not every organization responded to this message, but the ones they most wanted to convince did. Initially, Albertson recruited three national veterans' organizations and one local organization. When the foundation realized the smaller local organization was unable to keep pace with the others, it was replaced.

The three national nonprofits are groups that come up repeatedly in this book: Hire Heroes USA. Team Red, White, and Blue. And Team Rubicon.

Hire Heroes USA is the employment pillar. It offers a combination of one-on-one job coaching for veterans and spouses, group workshops focused on employment for individuals leaving the military, and cultivation of employers. The nonprofit decided to sign on after some initial hesitation because, as COO Nate Smith explains, "we discovered that the underemployment rate for veterans in Idaho was actually quite high. That information, combined with JKAF's unique ability to influence the Idaho market, was an attractive proposition for us."

Team Red, White, and Blue builds camaraderie and mutual-support networks among veterans, organized around physical fitness and social life. Its chapter-based approach helps veterans befriend others in their area, keeps them fit, connects them to other community members, and overcomes some of the feeling of isolation that many new veterans say is the strongest feeling early in civilian life, after the intense teamwork of military service.

Team Rubicon, which organizes veterans to respond to disasters, has clear practical value in a state vulnerable to forest fires. It also builds the esprit de corps that helps vets keep the best of their military experience alive, and hones skills that can be useful to emergency-medical services and fire departments in a far-flung state.

Finally, the Albertson Foundation recruited Guild Education, a private company, to help veterans and military spouses make it to and through college. The company provides college counseling for students seeking the right schools for their needs, and "intrusive advising" throughout their education to make sure they stay on track.

Mission 43

Beyond inviting these groups to expand to Idaho, the Albertson Foundation asked them to work together in what Johnston calls an "ecosystem" where each organization pursues its own specialties, but coordinates with the others. They called it Mission 43, a nod to Idaho's status as the 43rd state to join the Union. The ecosystem isn't designed to be all-encompassing. The goal is emphatically not to address every potential veteran need, or to try to squeeze every service provider dealing with veterans under one roof. Rather, Albertson aims to help a small number of highly capable and philosophically aligned organizations make Idaho a great place for veterans to thrive and contribute to their state. As Johnston put it, "These organizations are excellent because they are focused on mastering certain tasks. We don't ask them to do anything differently, we just ask that they do it in Idaho."

Here's what participation in the ecosystem means:

- *Funding.* After each organization sets goals with Albertson, the foundation provides it with the resources needed to get the job done. There is no competition between the groups.
- *Marketing.* Albertson provides professional marketing so each nonprofit can advertise the opportunities and services it offers across the wide spaces of rural Idaho.
- *Cross-referrals.* Leaders in each organization are trained on what the other partners provide, and are responsible for making referrals to one another wherever needed.
- *Institutional support.* Albertson provides its imprimatur as the major philanthropy in the state, which lends legitimacy and network connections to each participating group and the overall Mission 43 effort.

Albertson recruited a director to oversee all foundation grants for veterans, while also keeping Mission 43 as a whole moving toward its goals. West Point graduate, helicopter pilot, and National Guardsman Bryan Madden was hired soon after the original Mission 43 partner organizations were selected. In a very unconventional structure for a grantmaker, Madden works alongside his grantees, in the same office. He's responsible for setting milestones and keeping track of progress, troubleshooting operational challenges, and overseeing projects that don't fall into any one group's purview yet benefit them all collectively.

For example, Madden supervises the marketing team responsible for publicizing Mission 43 and member groups. He runs regular meetings during which partner organizations synchronize calendars and eliminate conflicts. He identifies opportunities for piggybacking on one another's work.

Madden describes Mission 43 as a "team of teams." Every organization has its own area of specialty, but shares the same aspiration of creating broad opportunities for veterans in Idaho. Each participant's success and credibility is bound to the progress of Mission 43 as a whole.

Operating in rural America

Establishment and growth of new entities is never easy, and there can be particular challenges in a rural environment. The Mission 43 partners worked hard to find the right people for full-time staff positions across the state, and even harder to fill volunteer and part-time roles. Where there are fewer people, and a much lower density population, it can be hard to find talent. Mission 43 is hoping to change that with time.

Grantees also had to adjust to working at a distance from their national leadership, and in coordination with other groups. It helps to have the four organizations co-located at the Albertson office, where the Mission 43 team meets every other week, and regional leaders of the different groups convene twice per year to share information and learn what the others can offer.

> These organizations are excellent. We don't ask them to do anything differently, we just ask that they do it in Idaho.

The organizations had to adjust their operations to the realities of Idaho communities. Guild Education delivers its coaching over the phone and Internet, and its partner universities are top online colleges, so it adapted most easily. The job coaching provided by Hire Heroes USA is done in the same way, but the rural labor market presented its own challenges. The nonprofit had to identify potential employers in remote areas and build relationships with them, requiring "lots of shoe-leather work," as Madden put it.

Team RWB and Team Rubicon are built on face-to-face relationships, so they had to set up new chapters with volunteer leaders all around the state, and engage dispersed veterans through them. Compared to chapters in more densely populated areas, it is asking more of veterans to congregate for bike rides or training sessions if that requires substantial travel. Mission 43 decided to hone its efforts and build momentum in the more urbanized Boise area, where it is based, then expand outward. Mission 43 emphatically wants to engage veterans all across their rural state, however, so regional expansion will be a long-term priority. Building a critical mass of participating veterans will make this easier.

Tracking progress

Madden produces a one-page performance dashboard every month. In additional to membership totals and marketing efforts, he tracks broad measures of service quality and quantity for each organization. For Hire Heroes USA this includes the number of veterans hired, their starting salary, and the percentage in full-time rather than part-time jobs. Guild Education tallies student enrollments, the rates at which they stay enrolled instead of dropping out, and the time it takes veterans to complete degrees. Team RWB counts membership growth and numbers of personal interactions. These are all indicators the organizations track anyway, but Madden has pulled out the ones that matter most to Mission 43's success. Each of his reports presents color-coded year-to-date percentages indicating how close or far each group is from their goals, alongside progress toward the annual Mission 43 goals. At a glance, the whole team can see where they are on track, and where they need to redouble efforts.

These monthly snapshots feed into the longer-term plan Albertson has for Mission 43. In Year One, the focus is on setting the organizations up in Idaho, getting them used to working with one another, and establishing a foothold in Boise, the state's capital and largest city. Year Two is all about expansion—reaching out to more distant corners of the state and trying to provide the same high-quality experience and outcomes. Year Three adds attention to sustainability, and starts asking whether particular undertakings are making enough of a difference in the lives of veterans to justify their continuation and expansion.

The Albertson Foundation kicked off Mission 43 with a $2 million investment in four organizations, officially launching in early 2016. Within six months, 60 veterans had been hired at salaries averaging around $50,000, more than 500 had participated in 2,100 exercise sessions with Team RWB, and 700 veterans had officially joined Mission 43. In a state with 37,000 post-9/11 vets, that's a pretty good start, but there's a lot more to do.

Assets Not Victims:
The Heinz Foundation sees vets as a competitive advantage

With more than 4 million Americans having served in the U.S. military since the 9/11 attacks, it is inevitable that a certain percentage will encounter some difficulties during their subsequent transition to civilian life. Like some other philanthropists, leaders at the Heinz Endowments wanted to do something to help those individuals. They asked Rob Stephany, their program director for community and economic development, to come up with a response.

Stephany summarizes their thinking. "We're a regional foundation. We are both grantmakers and advocates. We set agendas and we drive them. Successful lives for local veterans was defined as a key competitive issue for our region, and that's why the board wanted to get into it. It was that simple and straightforward."

The head of the foundation made a crucial decision to approach veterans using an economic-development lens, not a human-services lens. That's why Stephany was asked to take the lead. His philanthropic specialty was to get people and neighborhoods to a point where they could compete in the marketplace, whether that meant helping individuals take up work, or developing property to stabilize neighborhoods.

Stephany had experience helping regional nonprofits build housing and economic-development programs. Putting together a grant portfolio for veterans, though, was something new and unfamiliar. Complicating matters was that fact that a very unhealthy narrative was dominating the national conversation about veterans. Rob kept hearing "talk about post-traumatic stress like it was a disabling scourge, like a virus. And the work of integrating vets into civilian life was presented like some social-service drain and human burden."

After Stephany met Megan Andros, a West Point graduate and former Army ordnance officer, he asked her to conduct some research, and to survey veterans recently returned to the western-Pennsylvania home region of the Heinz Endowments, to identify their needs. "The basic questions," says Andros, "were 'What does the population look like? What do existing resources look like? And are they effective?'" She ran focus groups with 130 veterans to gather initial information. Soon Stephany offered her a permanent position at Heinz.

"I think everyone was shocked at how large our local population of veterans is," recalls Andros. Nearly a quarter of a million veterans live in the immediate region, and over 37,000 of them are post-9/11 veterans. But more detailed information about the population was scant. Improving local knowledge on veterans would become an important part of the foundation's strategy.

Learning from missteps
Even before the endowment took up its methodical commitment to veterans, it had a couple of large grants in the pipeline that were based on the conventional wisdom many funders in the field were following. In 2013, Heinz funded a couple projects aimed at some of the psychological wounds that

media reports suggested were ubiquitous among veterans. These included a jobs program for veterans with disabilities, and a nature retreat run by older veterans who wanted to help younger veterans with PTSD.

Of the charities available to fund, recalls Andros, "the vast majority were geared toward helping veterans in crisis—both in the way they worked, and in the way they fundraised." Moreover, "they were trying to assist veterans from the Iraq-Afghanistan era in the same way Vietnam-era veterans had been approached." They were focused on individuals with the worst problems. And they didn't find many former servicemembers who wanted what they offered.

The programs funded by the Heinz grants were not well attended. And they seemed to engender a counterproductive sense of weakness and dependency. "They tried to do whatever they could to tell this generation of veterans that they were frail victims," notes Stephany.

> The older veterans' charities were geared toward vets in crisis, and didn't recognize differences in the Iraq-Afghanistan cohort. What they offered didn't match many of the talented individuals leaving service.

The endowment had to climb a steep learning curve. "Our assumption was that there must be a lot of veterans trying to connect with those resources, and they just weren't able," says Andros. So Heinz, like a large number of other funders across the country following advice that continues to be fashionable, poured money into setting up a website that aimed simply to connect needy vets with existing agencies and organizations claiming they could help.

It quickly became apparent, though, that just creating a central list wouldn't work. Any sort of "community collaboration"—as these trendy efforts were labeled—was only as good as the individual organizations that make it up. And the reality is, many of the government programs and sentimental charities aimed at vets are ineffective or even counterproductive. A much smarter effort was needed.

Facing these initial failures squarely, the Heinz Endowments immediately adjusted course. Andros's presence helped. She knew from her own experience in the Army that the conventional philanthropic approach to who veterans are and what they need didn't match the many talented, high-potential individuals coming out of our volunteer military. She knew the endowment, and the field generally, needed more accurate information on which to base decision-making. And she suspected that different parts of the country would have particular topics they'd need to address. "One-size-fits-all solutions and sweeping generalizations do a lot of damage. Every region has specific issues they have to deal with."

So Heinz commissioned a study of the needs of veterans in southwestern Pennsylvania, conducted by the Center for a New American Security. The result was a trove of useful data profiling local vets. Heinz learned details of demographics, employment and earnings levels, health status, and self-reported challenges.

It turned out that six out of ten new vets were entering civilian life without major problems, finding work and nestling into towns across the region. The situation was just the opposite for about 2 percent of the returning men and women. This small group had serious problems with addiction or homelessness or disability. Government V.A. resources were flowing heavily to that slice of the population.

The other 38 percent were folks who could be helped with small boosts. They had jobs, but not thriving careers, or missed the clear sense of purpose they felt while in the military. Given the right support at the right time, they had an excellent chance of succeeding.

Heinz sensed a big opportunity to do something with this latter group. In particular, it was interested in intervening with preventive programs before significant problems could gather together into a crisis. Stephany remembers realizing, "There's not a 'catch them before they fall' charity operating here. We think that is where philanthropic resources can best help." Andros agreed that helping veterans to thrive so as to get ahead of potential problems was the best way to make a lifelong impact on individuals and on Pennsylvania communities.

"It's not about fixing them"

This new approach required different ways of thinking, and a new set of nonprofit partners. "We went from approaching this as a charitable mission to understanding veterans as assets of generational importance, with our role being to help them migrate into civilian society in the most successful ways." Heinz asked old-line veterans' organizations to help them in this new approach, but didn't find any local groups willing to shift gears, or able to change fast enough. Then Andros met, at a Philanthro-py Roundtable conference, the leaders of several organizations breaking new ground in charitable work for veterans. What united these groups was the fact that they had tested and proved out the thesis that veterans are civic assets, not fodder for pity—and then built all of their program-ming on that important insight.

"It's not about fixing them. It's about having communities in the Pittsburgh area embrace their talent," says Andros. Building purpose and high expectations and community is the very best way to help most new veterans, savvy philanthropists are now finding.

Heinz approached The Mission Continues (see Chapter 11 in *Serving Those Who Served*), a national organization that provides six-month part-time service fellowships, and service platoons in which veterans are organized for volunteer work and camaraderie with the expectation that they will contin-ue to serve others in civilian life as they did in the military. Andros asked the group what roles vets might play in the economic-development work of the Heinz Endowments. The Mission Continues hadn't yet expanded to Pitts-burgh, but it seemed like a good fit geographically, so the nonprofit prepared a proposal to organize a local service platoon of several dozen veterans under a platoon leader it would recruit. Andros would help that person find the right project in Pittsburgh where both the veterans and the service recipients would benefit from the effort.

The first mission they settled on was helping low-income elderly live independently in their homes. By repairing houses of older people too infirm to do it themselves and too poor to hire a contractor, neighbor-hoods would be helped at the same time that veterans found purpose and community in meaningful volunteer work with other veterans. It was a perfect fit.

Stephany describes an average project: "They come on a Saturday, 30-strong, and walk door to door with neighborhood partners. They help senior citizens clean out their basement, or fix a leaky pipe, or clear a fire hazard." When delivered with the consistency and discipline of a service platoon, seemingly small projects like these make a world of dif-ference for both residents and veterans finding their way in a new world. This initial project was so successful that another neighborhood group asked The Mission Continues to organize a second service platoon. Both are now active in the Pittsburgh area.

At this point, local community organizations started to pick up on the ways that Heinz was promoting veterans. Leadership Pittsburgh, a group devoted to training and connecting local leaders, took an interest and joined Andros in producing a six-month-long course for veterans that teaches them about the region and its challenges, introduces them to civic heads and business executives, and helps place them on service and nonprofit boards around the city. After three cohorts of 20 veterans had gone through the course, veterans were more engaged in the region and bringing new energy to community positions. And more stable gradu-ates of the program were informally mentoring some of the younger and less settled participants who were struggling to find direction and good jobs after service.

The data that Heinz collected early on suggested that some young veterans in their area were employed for fewer hours than they wanted to work, and at wages lower than they should be able to command. And despite good intentions, most of the existing organizations addressing jobs for veterans were part of the problem. As Andros explains, they were "all organized to help the lowest common denominator in crisis get a job, not a career. What happens when you're fully capable of a career and you enroll in an organization that can only get you a job? Now you're 'at risk.'"

> It's not about fixing them. It's about having communities in the Pittsburgh area embrace their talent.

Heinz needed a partner that better understood the capacities of young post-9/11 veterans and how to help them succeed occupationally. Andros likes to say she "stole" the idea of using Corporate America Supports You from fellow funder Dan Goldenberg at the Call of Duty Endowment. Based on the audit of CASY done by Call of Duty, Andros thought the national job-aid organization might be a good match for what she needed. So she called it up and said, "I love what you're doing nationally, but can you focus it on these three counties in southwestern Pennsylvania, and focus on under-employment rather than just joblessness?" The nonprofit decided that with some adjustments, it could be done.

Stephany likes the fact that CASY works from both ends of the employment contract. "They build relationships with employers. They partner with hiring managers of firms and help mold, change, and challenge job descriptions to better match corporate opportunities and vets." And in their interactions with former servicemembers they ask jobseekers to "look into their souls and find out what they really want to do. They match that with what their CV ought to look like, given the experience they have. They don't want to place somebody and have them leave after six months because they don't like where they are."

Both CASY and Heinz want to help veterans enter long-term vocations, not just jobs. And their collaboration seems to be working. As of May 2016, less than a year into its first grant, CASY has placed 200 veterans in jobs in the Pittsburgh area, with a median annual salary of $50,000.

A network backbone

To help local veterans find these new services it was creating, the Heinz Endowments gave the Syracuse University Institute for Veterans and Military Families a grant to create a new organization known as PA Serves. "Simply put, it's a concierge service," says Andros. The group helps direct veterans to programs they are interested in and qualified for, and it helps organizations refer their participants to other Heinz grantees. A small staff coordinates the linkups, and keeps track of interactions between individuals and organizations, including sending customer-service messages to veterans to gather feedback. Every organization joining the network has to commit to sharing information and participants with one another.

PA Serves makes it easy for service groups to refer vets to other organizations for needs outside their area of expertise. With just a few clicks they can send requests to others in the network, then get back to what they do best. In its first year, PA Serves connected 933 vets with over 1,600 services.

One unanticipated side benefit of the information-sharing that PA Serves makes so much easier is that it exposes the small number of clients who are just aimlessly fishing for benefits. "One of the interesting early findings of the network was that many of the first folks to put in service requests had been seen multiple times by other participating nonprofits," says Stephany. "They were people working the system for whatever resources they could find, without putting much effort of their own in. Now all of that was transparent to several dozen charities."

Initially, Stephany was skeptical of the bureaucracy that often accompanies large collaborations. "I think 147 different nonprofits in Allegheny County mention veterans in their mission statement. We invited them all to our initial meeting. We told them openness and accountability were essential to us. About 40 showed up at the next meeting. Among the several dozen groups in our network today, only a small number are specifically focused on veterans. The rest are just great regional nonprofits."

In addition to offering veterans a wide range of employment, health, family, financial, and other services, the information shared across this network has provided a steady deepening of understanding of the needs of local veterans, helping Heinz and other charitable funders recognize trends on which to make future grants. For example, says Andros, "right now, older veterans age 45 to 64 are requesting housing support and financial assistance. Younger post-9/11 veterans are requesting education planning, social networking, and volunteering opportunities. So now I can say to an organization, 'wait a second, if you're supporting post-9/11 vets, you need to be in these areas.'"

Within the first few years of deciding to make support for veterans a permanent part of its charitable work in western Pennsylvania, the Heinz Endowments had become masterful in studying and understanding the real needs of local veterans. Then it invested $4.3 million over its first three years, learned from mistakes, and made sure it got the results it wanted. In the process it has recast the veterans of its region as civic assets. By carefully testing out ways of providing early support, it is helping even vulnerable vets avoid crises down the road, while helping the large mass of men and women who need only small nudges of assistance to develop into thriving and productive citizens.

Don't Patronize—Empower:
Bernie Marcus makes veterans self-reliant

Bernie Marcus became a business icon by reimagining American home improvement. Rather than limiting homeowners to a smaller selection of goods at neighborhood hardware stores and professional contractors to separate wholesale outlets, he tapped into the burgeoning do-it-yourself movement in America and offered a huge array of building materials to all. His store, Home Depot, treated every shopper like a professional contractor—goods were stacked on pallets in massive warehouses, and frills were few. But prices were deeply discounted.

Marcus and his partners opened two locations in Atlanta in 1979, then grew their business into an international empire. Needing an army of associates in orange aprons to keep the operation humming, and having a patriot's appreciation for the U.S. military, Marcus and company established veteran-friendly business practices. Today, about 10 percent of Home Depot employees are either veterans or military Reservists. If any of those Reservists are called up and paid less in the military than they would have earned at Home Depot, the company pays the difference while they are on duty.

In addition to being a serious friend to veterans, Marcus and his family have been some of the most generous philanthropists in America. Marcus gave $250 million to create the Georgia Aquarium as a gift to the Atlanta-area workers and customers who initially made Home Depot succeed. He founded Autism Speaks and transformed autism from painful mystery to widely understood and treated condition. And Marcus made very large gifts to medical facilities in the Atlanta area and Florida.

Support for veterans and servicemembers became a priority for Marcus starting in 2007. As he throttled back his involvement in his company and became more engaged in giving his fortune away, he wanted to support veterans coming home from the wars in Iraq and Afghanistan. In a few short years, he would invest over $40 million in assistance for veterans, with much more to come.

Advanced care for brain injuries

While touring the Shepherd Center in 2007, a nationally prominent rehabilitation hospital in Atlanta that he had been supporting for years, Marcus met a young soldier with a spinal-cord injury (Shepherd's specialty) and a traumatic brain injury (TBI). He was astonished to learn that although the soldier was stationed at a base just an hour and a half away, and had been given a prognosis of paralysis from the waist down for the rest of his life, he had been waiting months for the military to process his paperwork and discharge him to V.A. care.

The man had exited his bureaucratic limbo only because his family became involved and found the specialized services of the Shepherd Center. There the doctors were much more optimistic about his chances of rehabilitation. Within three weeks, the soldier was up and walking.

The episode left Marcus deeply moved. And agitated. Marcus Ruzek, an Army Reservist who directs Marcus's veterans' giving, explains that "Bernie concluded that the Defense Department and V.A. are failing on spinal cord injury and traumatic brain injury. He wanted to make sure that any servicemembers and veterans who needed it could have access to top civilian medical care like that offered at the Shepherd Center."

Marcus offered Shepherd $2 million in seed funding and a challenge to build up a program where servicemembers and veterans with traumatic brain injuries could get intensive treatment. The specialists at Shepherd created what they called their SHARE initiative. It opened its doors in 2008.

When they arrive in Atlanta, SHARE participants undergo a two-week assessment of their symptoms and functional limitations, led by a team of neurologists, psychiatrists, psychologists, speech pathologists, and physical therapists. They produce a set of treatment recommendations. The patient then undergoes 8 to 12 weeks of intensive therapy. In additional to their medical treatment, participants work with recreational therapists, social workers, and vocational rehabilitation experts. The goal is improved daily functioning leading to independence. After veterans return home, a SHARE case manager orchestrates 12 to 24 months of follow-up. If more treatment is needed, the patient returns to the Shepherd Center.

The SHARE program stands in stark contrast to other forms of brain-injury treatment available to veterans. First, it is intensive and full-time—patients live in nearby apartments for months while they spend eight hours a day, five days a week, plus weekends, working on getting healthy. "In SHARE," Ruzek notes, "you're immersed." Second, the clinicians are from several fields, highly skilled in brain injuries, and dedicated entirely to SHARE, not split among different departments in a larger hospital.

The program accepts participants on a rolling basis, with space for up to ten at a time (50 patients per year). "And you're in a culture of people getting better. So the incentive to actually get better and move on and get to the next stage of your life is there," says Ruzek.

As an example of the 300 or so lives that SHARE has changed, Ruzek cites a soldier injured by a blast in Iraq. She returned home to a child, but needed a caretaker even to attend to her own needs. Her husband got frustrated and left her before she came to SHARE as a last-ditch option. By the time she had completed the program she was able to hold a job, live without a caretaker, and regain custody of her daughter.

SHARE results are publicly available. They show consistent improvement on most measures of debilitating medical symptoms—headache and dizziness, pain, PTSD and depression, and difficulty sleeping. The program also tracks positive effects like return to work or school, and personal goals met.

Despite its clear successes, Bernie Marcus was dissatisfied with one important aspect of the program. At one prominent public event, Ruzek says, his outspoken boss "got up as the keynote speaker and said, 'You know, this is a great program. But it's a failure because we've never found a way to replicate it so it can do its good for an even larger number of people.' That has always been his frustration."

Starting in 2010, after SHARE showed promising results, Marcus organized meetings with Defense Department officials, V.A. leaders, and the U.S. Surgeon General's office to allow the team from SHARE to explain their work and offer to treat more veterans and servicemembers. According to Ruzek, "they all agreed it was great, and that there was no reason the government agencies couldn't work together to get more veterans this superb care. And then all collaboration completely fell apart after the meeting."

> He concluded that the Defense Department and V.A. are failing on spinal-cord injury and brain injuries.

The experience left a bad taste in Marcus's mouth. In one 2015 television interview he leveled a straightforward judgment: "I think the V.A. is the most disgraceful organization in America today. If it were a private institution it would be bankrupt and closed. Our wounded warriors deserve much more than they're getting."

Rather than let bureaucratic incompetence stop him, Marcus trimmed the scope of his ambitions, then continued his philanthropic work to provide superior care without V.A. support. Patients continue to stream into SHARE by word of mouth referrals from knowledgeable veterans and doctors. And the program has a waiting list.

Though it doesn't charge veterans or servicemembers anything, the SHARE program is financially stable. After Marcus covered the startup costs of setting up offices, hiring a team, and developing the program, SHARE settled into a budget of about $1.2 million per year. The program receives partial reimbursements from insurance companies covering about 10 percent of its costs. The rest comes from local philanthropy.

A giant end-run around government obstacles

Deeply frustrated by his experience with the V.A., Bernie Marcus stepped away from brain-injury work for several years. SHARE continued at a steady state, but no expansion was contemplated. Eventually, Marcus decided he wanted to try again to improve brain-injury treatment for veterans.

After deciding he needed someone to focus full-time on his veterans' giving, Bernie Marcus hired Marcus Ruzek in 2013. Ruzek had no background in nonprofit or foundation work, so Marcus first had him learn his values and study his giving philosophy, so he could stay true to donor intent. Then he asked Ruzek to overlay this new philanthropic knowledge with his own experience with soldiers and veterans, which included three tours in Iraq and Afghanistan, and the government bureaucracies serving them. Ruzek put together a series of grants to solid veterans' groups. (More on these later.)

Then Marcus gave Ruzek a very clear order. "I want you to make SHARE a nationwide network, and really extend it. Go big."

This would be a long-term project. As Ruzek notes, "brain injury is a complex issue, with institutional obstacles we had already encountered, so we couldn't responsibly step out and make a major grant right away." But Ruzek started talking with experts at SHARE, and others in the field, about opportunities to improve concussion and brain-injury care, in light of what was available at the V.A. and Defense Department facilities.

Ruzek visited other examples of excellent medical philanthropy for veterans, like Operation Mend, the surgery program for severely injured vets (see Case Study Nine in *Serving Those Who Served*). Ruzek met Dr. Jim Kelly, the founding director of NICoE, the medical facility launched by philanthropist Arnold Fisher and his family to create excellent brain-injury treatment through the Department of Defense (see Case Study Eight in *Serving Those Who Served*).

Kelly had been treating brain injury among accident victims, professional athletes, and veterans for decades by the time he met Ruzek. He pointed out that "85 percent of concussions heal without much being done. You monitor them, keep patients from repeating the damage, and they tend to recover." The 15 percent of patients who didn't naturally recover were a bit of a mystery. Doctors were more focused on addressing symptoms than tackling root causes.

Early in his career, Kelly had focused on treating the much tinier number of patients suffering severe or penetrating brain injuries. He applied those principles to the patients with milder injuries, concussions, who weren't recovering, and found subtle versions of the same problems he saw in more severe brain injury. This gave him specific targets to treat.

Though NICoE had special prerogatives to cut through red tape, it was still part of the military health system, which limited its flexibility. It could only treat servicemembers, not veterans, and it lacked adequate capacity to be a national solution. Ruzek and some outside consultants he hired examined other mental-health and brain-injury clinics for veterans popping up around the country, weighing their pros and cons, but none seemed to provide the broad solution Bernie Marcus was looking for.

Then in 2015 Dr. Kelly decided that if he wanted to bring the intensive NICoE-style approach to repairing brain injuries to the maximum number of patients he would have to do that in the private sector. Exiting the military health system would make it easier for him to collaborate with other medical leaders, and allow him to serve veterans, where the lion's share of today's need lies. Working in a more flexible environment, preferably an academic medical center, would also allow him to teach, contribute to much-needed research in the field, and spread intensive approaches to concussion care more easily.

Together, Ruzek and Kelly started working on a plan to build a preeminent brain-injury clinic. It would be located on the Anschutz Campus of the University of Colorado School of Medicine, Kelly's home teaching institution. And it would offer the best concussion care for a thousand miles in any direction.

To control expenses so the program would be viable to expand widely, Kelly planned to decrease staff and share more equipment with other clinics at the hospital, compared to the NICoE model. But the integrity of his program remains the same—it lasts four weeks, focusing intently on diagnostics and development of an individualized treatment plan. Patients start their treatment on-site, and then transition to their home communities to continue rehabilitation.

Initially, the Colorado clinic will serve around 400 patients per year. Veterans will receive care alongside elite athletes, civilian car-crash victims, and injured workers. Kelly believes this will be helpful in normalizing understandings of brain injury, and speeding and mainstreaming the recovery of veterans.

As with the SHARE program, the Marcus Foundation and Kelly are committed to ensuring no veteran will pay for care at this clinic. Their business plan calls for seeking reimbursement from private insurers and government where available, generating revenue from their treatment of private civilian cases and athletes, renting out use of their high-end diagnostic equipment to other hospital departments, seeking grants for research, and filling financial gaps with philanthropy. On an annual operating budget of $6 million, they expect to be able to reduce their need for philanthropic support to under $1 million annually within a period of years.

Bernie Marcus has made it clear to Ruzek that he would consider opening just one clinic, no matter how good, a failure. He wants a national network that can help thousands of veterans per year. So a plan has been launched, with backing from other philanthropists, to make Kelly's clinic at the University of Colorado a hub that works closely with SHARE and other clinics around the country. These sites will share knowledge and clinical approaches, collaborate on research, and direct patients in any region of the country to the most appropriate clinic site.

The network aims to serve around 2,000 veterans per year. A research organization has joined the alliance to manage and share the reams of data the clinics will produce. It's called OneMind, and is run, with philanthropic support, by Pete Chiarelli, former vice chief of staff of the Army.

Satisfied with this ambitious proposal, Bernie Marcus signed off on a grant to launch Jim Kelly's clinic at the University of Colorado, a commitment over $30 million, in addition to a sizable promise to integrate other medical facilities into the network. At the same time, Marcus invested $3.8 million to purchase a building that will allow SHARE to double its annual capacity to 100 patients, as its contribution to this burgeoning network.

Donors and service providers alike often lament the lack of collaboration between different efforts serving the same populations. Ruzek made common cause with other donors early on, sharing each revision of the plan, and looking for opportunities to work together. In Colorado, for instance, he consulted with local funders like the Anschutz Foundation, Daniels Fund, El Pomar Foundation, and Sturm Family Foundation. Nationally, he kept in touch with leaders of the Cohen Veterans Network (more on that later). As one result, patients will be freely referred back and forth between the programs focusing on mental health and those concentrating on brain injury. With donors like these involved early on, there's a high chance we'll see sizable partnerships in the future.

Independence for the catastrophically injured

Casualty rates have declined dramatically over the last century of American warfare. In World War I, more than 6,700 fighters out of every 100,000 were injured or killed. By the time of the Iraq and Afghanistan wars that rate had dropped to 912. In the world's best-trained and best-equipped military, battlefield injuries are increasingly rare. And for those who do get injured, survival rates have increased from 64 percent to 88 percent over that same period.

The dark side of this trend is that some survivors today live with grievous physical effects that forever change the way they go about daily life. Out of about 2.5 million servicemembers deployed, the Iraq and Afghanistan wars have left about 1,600 individuals with limb amputations, 990 severely burned, and several hundred with spinal-cord injuries. That isn't an exhaustive list of life-altering wounds, but it gives a sense of the number of catastrophically injured persons meriting the nation's attention.

A substantial portion of Bernie Marcus's giving focuses on this small but vitally needy and deserving population of veterans. In particular, he has committed $8.5 million to build 27 custom smart homes for some of our most severely wounded servicemembers and their families. He works with two charities—the Gary Sinise Foundation, and the Stephen Siller Tunnel-to-Towers Foundation—that have particular specialties in this niche.

A number of charities have given away mortgage-free homes to veterans over the last decade. Often these will be foreclosed homes donated by banks and then renovated for the recipient. Eligibility is usually based on having a V.A. disability rating of a certain level, regardless of whether the disability creates specific functional limitations like climbing stairs. These home giveaways put roofs over the heads of some veterans and their families as a deep expression of gratitude, but few were tightly targeted to the needs of veterans with the most barriers to independent living.

The Sinise and Siller organizations are different. They are aimed specifically, Ruzek notes, at "the very severely wounded population—triple amputees, victims burned over 80 percent of their bodies, those with severe brain injuries who will need full-time caretakers for the rest of their lives. The first home that Siller built was for the first quadruple amputee to ever survive a war. He happened to be from Staten Island,

New York, near where the foundation is based, and so they built his home. That's how they got started."

The small bit of good news in this sad situation, says Ruzek, is that "this population is in the hundreds. It's not thousands or tens of thousands. We look at it as a solvable problem. Every severely wounded veteran from Iraq and Afghanistan who needs a smart home to live independently can get one within the next few years."

Building each home is a major undertaking because it has to be designed to accommodate the serious limitations of the veteran. Everything gets adjusted, from ramps and elevators, to adaptive showers and oversized light switches, to cabinets and countertops that raise or lower at the push of a button. No detail is too small for these two charities. As Siller home recipient Todd Nicely put it, "the biggest things in this home are the smallest ones."

> Marcus considers opening just one clinic a failure. He wants a national network that can help thousands of veterans a year.

The Siller and Sinise foundations act as project managers. They find veterans who qualify, oversee the design, raise all of the funds for the project, supervise the building process, then make sure the vet settles well in the new house.

Great effort is exerted to make sure the home creates independence and empowerment for the veteran, not a message of "we feel really bad for you, here's a house—just stay in there." Once vets get into their homes, the first question asked is how they plan to give back. They are particularly encouraged to help other vets trailing them in the recovery process.

The cost of these houses generally ranges from $600,000 to $700,000. This gets reduced by in-kind support from manufacturers who subsidize components. For Siller houses, MasterBrand provides cabinetry, HunterDouglas does the window treatments, and Carpet One provides floor covering, among others. Separately from Bernie Marcus's giving, the Home Depot contributes both direct funding and in-kind donations to both organizations, along with volunteer time from store associates. Local donors provide further help. And the V.A. will cover up to $70,000 for adaptive housing, though it requires a complex application that the charities help the beneficiaries put together.

By the time the Marcus Foundation and other major funders come in as the final funders, the gap needing to be filled is much reduced. The Siller Foundation, for instance, was able to complete 14 homes using just $150,000 each of Marcus Foundation support in its last grant cycle. Says Ruzek of these two partners, "they're each now doing 15, 16 homes a year. So this issue will be solved in a few years."

Helping everyday vets thrive

Because Marcus Ruzek is still in the Army Reserve, and because his boss had been fairly quiet in his giving to veterans, Ruzek has often been able to experience charities for vets as a participant, without being identified as the representative of a major philanthropist, at least for a little while. He joined a number of organizations as a regular member to see what participants experience. He kept asking himself, "Is this something I think is worth my time? Is this something that could help me if I were struggling?"

In addition to looking at management and business practices, and considering whether the organization would be a good steward of Marcus Foundation resources, Ruzek developed a litmus test he considers important to the success and self-respect of veterans. He decided he would ask every potential grantee not just what it could offer to veterans, but "what it would require of them. What do you ask them to do in return? We're trying to reinforce the fact that veterans aren't broken, that they aren't charity cases. Veterans are actually a great part of our society who can give back if empowered to do so. They will integrate faster, be better citizens, and recover from any setbacks more completely if you require them to put effort into their own advancement, and into helping others."

Viewed with these sorts of factors in mind, Ruzek soon zeroed in on a number of charities that are now major players, but which were just starting to expand and professionalize when he started investigating them. These include Team Red, White, and Blue; The Mission Continues; and Team Rubicon. The Marcus Foundation played a crucial role in fueling the growth of these three from brand-new concepts of how to minister to vets, to their current positions as thriving charities of first-rank effectiveness.

"What every one of those organizations does is pull veterans out of social isolation and into a community with comrades and those who have had similar experiences. They all require hard things of their participants. And they all write their members into a larger and very inspiring story, which is the same thing that happened to them in the military," says Ruzek.

"We found these groups to be a very, very important piece of the transition to civilian life, and of strong and balanced mental health. If you can put social supports and protective factors around transitioning veterans of exactly the sort that these organizations supply, then most of them are not going to be at risk."

Beyond cutting checks to these organizations, the Marcus Foundation helped shaped their structures. Take, for example, Team Red, White, and Blue. The basic thesis of the organization goes something like this: If you bring veterans, servicemembers, and civilians together through regular physical and social activity, their lives and relationships will be enriched in ways that will help them weather challenges.

Impressed with Team RWB's model, and particularly with its leadership, the Marcus Foundation decided to fund the organization's growth. Relying on volunteers, it had already grown organically to 40,000 members nationwide. The foundation offered Team RWB a $1.3 million grant to expand across the Southeast. This paid for a marketing and branding campaign, hired staff, and more programming. The group expected 15 percent annual growth. Instead, regional membership more than doubled in less than a year, from 7,600 to 17,800. Team RWB became the fastest-growing veterans' organization in the country, and now has over 120,000 members.

In 2016, the Marcus Foundation expanded its pilot investment with another $4.8 million over three years. Most of this is committed to program delivery; some goes to improving the group's technology infrastructure and evaluation capacity—it needs tools to track what's happening at mushrooming chapters, to make sure they remain responsive to their members.

Less than a year after its first Team RWB grant, the Marcus Foundation invested $2.5 million in Team Rubicon's growth along the Atlantic seaboard. The money was aimed at expanding enrollment, engagement, and community impact—within this organization that mobilizes veterans to respond to disasters. Its model has two goals: Help individuals and communities traumatized by events beyond anyone's control. And offer veterans a sense of purpose and civilian usefulness. The Marcus Foundation was impressed at its demonstrated ability to achieve both of these objectives, in a variety of mobilizations in many different places.

Last, the Marcus Foundation put substantial funding into The Mission Continues to bring that group, which organizes veterans for community-service projects, to Atlanta. After an initial $50,000 grant to form a local service platoon yielded double the expected participation, the foundation decided to ramp up—offering an additional $680,000 over three years. This launched three more platoons, and funded 12 fellowships placing trained veterans in nonprofits around the Atlanta area.

By replacing the strong teamwork and purpose that many veterans miss when they leave the military, these groups help many former servicemembers shift gears to a productive civilian life. "We're measuring through surveys that their lives are more enriched, they have greater sense of purpose, and they have a better connection into their community. The problem with a lot of veterans is that they get out of the military and their entire support network is gone. If they move to some new place, or even if they move back home, they're a changed person and they don't have any network to lean on. That's what these groups offer. By connecting new arrivals with people already entrenched in the city, they also become natural referral services."

Going Big:
Steve Cohen spends heavily on mental health

In the brick and glass headquarters of Point72 Asset Management, hedge-fund analysts struggle night and day to place good bets. In amongst the many talented individuals sits Anthony Hassan, who spent most of his career as an Air Force social worker. From his bio he seems like a fish out of water amongst the economists and traders and math whizzes. But just like everyone else in the building, Hassan is trying to crack codes, solve complex problems, and build models that will generate reliable returns. Although he is not a trader, Hassan's success is as important to Point72 CEO Steve Cohen as that of any of the firm's money managers. The only difference is that while the other executives are charged with making money, Anthony's job is to give away $325 million—in ways that improve the lives of veterans and military families.

With more than $11 billion under management, Point72 relies on analytical rigor to achieve good results. So does the Cohen Veterans Network. But there is an additional emotional element to CVN. Steve Cohen's son Robert decided to enlist in the Marines after graduating from Brown University in 2007. With his country fighting in Afghanistan and Iraq, Robert felt called to serve.

"Like many parents who hear this in a time of war, I was shocked," says the elder Cohen. But he describes the day he watched his son graduate from boot camp on Parris Island as "the proudest in his life." Robert soon deployed to Afghanistan.

Robert returned from overseas in good health. Certain of his comrades, however, did not. A few came home with PTSD. Some had trouble coping when they made the transition from mission-centered, team-oriented military life to the much more atomized existence of civilian society. Hearing these stories from his son, Cohen became concerned that the nation was not doing enough to support some veterans.

Building on what he already knew

Cohen began to look for ways he could make a difference. He was already involved with the New York City-based Robin Hood Foundation, where he helped raise $13 million earmarked for veteran-related causes. (For details on this portfolio, see Case Four in *Serving Those Who Served*.) In 2012, Cohen chaired a special advisory board to oversee how the Robin Hood funds would be disbursed. The board focused on three issues: employment, homelessness, and mental health.

Within 18 months of making its grants to a range of New York City charities, Robin Hood was seeing indications of progress in the areas of homelessness and employment. But their efforts to strengthen mental health among veterans and their families seemed only to be scratching the surface. As Cohen adviser Michael Sullivan explained, "we had neither the resources, nor the partners, nor the infrastructure, or really any of the pieces to deal with veteran mental health in a systematic way. There was no hospital or other institution where you could write a check and say, 'Help us with this.'"

While the V.A. was offering care, it wasn't available in a timely or convenient way. Bureaucracy, waits, and concerns about losing cash disability benefits if they exhibited signs of improvement kept some veterans away from the V.A. Others didn't have the option to use V.A. services—like veterans with discharges for bad conduct, and family members of veterans. There are publicly funded community mental-health centers around the country, but only some are specially equipped to serve veterans. And many medical professionals who would have liked to help veterans and their families had no mechanism for getting reimbursed for services in the face of V.A. service monopolies.

To Cohen and his team it seemed clear that new mechanisms for delivering mental-health services to veterans were needed. He was prepared to provide enough resources to dent the problem, but, first, fresh institutions and leadership were needed. He asked his management team to provide options.

In 2013, Cohen's first move was to fund a pilot program—a clinic at New York University for military families. This had been initiated by the Robin Hood fund, but Cohen subsequently took full responsibility for funding it. His initial grant of $6.8 million over five years was a way to do immediate good while giving his team a chance to explore the larger problem and learn how to deliver high-quality, no-cost mental health care in a nonprofit setting. This initial funding also supported advanced research by the clinic's director, Charles Marmar, that attempted to identify clear biomarkers indicating that a patient was experiencing post-traumatic stress. Since the first creation of PTSD as a psychological diagnosis, attempts to treat the malady have been plagued by the fact that it relies completely on self-reported symptoms, with no reliable biological signs existing to definitively show whether the disorder exists, and whether it is waning or deepening.

While Marmar's research had clear value, the early results at the treatment clinic weren't as encouraging. It was hitting its minimum numbers for patient enrollment, but was nowhere near full capacity—and the team knew there were patients out there who needed help. As Sullivan noted, "One of the things we learned was that there is a lot of outreach required to find and enroll vets in need of treatment." The NYU clinic launched a social-media campaign, recruited through local veterans' organizations, and embedded representatives at the local V.A. hospital to find patients.

It learned that the key to getting veterans to enter PTSD treatment, and stick with it for the 12 to 15 sessions that are the standard therapy, is to involve family members. This came to distinguish the Cohen clinic from others, including the V.A., that don't offer care linking veterans, spouses, and children alike. By 2015, the NYU clinic had worked out the kinks and was treating over 350 families a year. And the treatment was making a difference.

Time for a big bet

Satisfied that the clinic in New York was learning how to do things right, and disgusted with steady media reports of poor care and long waiting lists at V.A. hospitals, Steve Cohen felt the time had come to dramatically expand the ambitions of his philanthropic project. He commissioned Bridgespan, a consulting firm for nonprofits, to develop a strategy for opening a whole network of philanthropic mental health clinics for veterans all across the county. He had two goals: 1) Help veterans and their families right away. 2) Seek better diagnostics and more effective remedies that could put treatment of the very slippery but wrenching syndrome of PTSD on a more solid basis in the long term.

> The key to getting veterans to enter PTSD treatment and stick with it is to involve family members. This distinguishes the Cohen clinic.

In practical terms, Cohen committed to building a network of up to 25 national clinics, while funding a major research effort on brain disorders and mental health. These two efforts would become known as the Cohen Veterans Network (CVN) and Cohen Veterans Bioscience (CVB). Although the two organizations are independent, data from the CVN clinics will shape the direction of CVB research, and scientific breakthroughs will be put to work immediately with clinic patients. As Hassan explains, "This is an ideal partnership where we can seamlessly go from bench science to implementation in the field, with no impeding bureaucracy."

To manage the ambitious clinic effort, Cohen hired Anthony Hassan in 2015. Hassan had co-founded and run the Center for Innovation and Research on Veterans & Military Families at the University of Southern California. He was asked to open four new clinics by the end of 2016. This involved creating a rubric for selecting which cities should get clinics, identifying local partners, hiring staff, establishing protocols for care, recruiting local philanthropists willing to share costs, developing a national marketing campaign, managing data, and creating a plan for financial sustainability. Hassan's position is a hybrid—part grantmaker, part operator of a health-care network. And the nonprofit he steers is structured as an entity separate from, but funded directly by, the Steven and Alexandra Cohen Foundation.

Practical details

Careful thought was given to the structure of the clinics. They provide extensive screening on the same day patients are enrolled, and promise a first therapeutic appointment within one week. Clinicians are trained specifically to work with veterans. In addition to their medical services, clinics can connect patients to resources for jobs, housing, financial literacy, and education.

One misconception of military and veteran mental health is that all patients have PTSD. The reality is that only about 20 percent of the people who enter the Cohen Veterans Network come in with that condition. The other 80 percent are treated for conditions like depression, anxiety, anger, bereavement, and marital and family issues. Contrary to the trendy narrative that traumatic stress is the "signature wound of the war on terror," the reality is that only a modest number of new veterans have had any experience of traumatic stress as a disorder.

The CVN mission is to provide care to as many post-9/11 veterans and their families as possible. With this in mind, the clinics do not treat the chronically mental ill, because that would crowd out the larger population. Patients with chronic mental illnesses are referred to specialized settings. "We are here to serve veterans and military families who present for care, receive care in a dozen or so sessions, and then go out and live healthier, happier lives." This matches the best medical understandings of even conditions like PTSD—which is in nearly all cases quite treatable, not a permanent affliction.

To decide where to locate clinics, Hassan cross-referenced data on where veterans live in the greatest numbers with information on where there is the most unmet need, where good resources already exist, and good intel on where helpful allies might be found. Since CVN does not allocate money for buildings, Hassan has to find organizations—usually hospitals, universities, or community health clinics—to host its programs. He usually conducts two roundtable discussions with potential partners in communities he is considering. One is with local medical professionals, fraternal groups, and military officials. A second roundtable gathers veterans, family members, and community caregivers. The CVN board makes the final decision on siting.

At each clinic, CVN collects three basic categories of data. First, it tracks structural outcomes—whether patients have access, whether the marketing is working, how many new patients are coming through the doors. Second, utilization rates, types of patients, conditions treated, type of care provided, and costs. Finally, CVN measures outcomes. "We look at patient satisfaction, time in care, and provider satisfaction. We compare results of the initial intake screenings when patients begin their treatment, halfway through treatment, and then at the end of treatment," notes Hassan. "These intake screeners look at things like sleep quality, relationships, well-being, suicidal thoughts, and so forth."

Electronic health records are mandated at every CVN clinic, because they are the only way to quickly cycle data from clinicians to researchers. CVN personnel have immediate access to a trove of anonymized traumatic-stress and mental-health information. If a researcher discovers a potential diagnostic or therapy, he or she can initiate a pilot study to confirm the possible link. "If the pilot study seems effective, we can easily conduct a broader study across the entire network without extensive bureaucratic barriers impeding progress. We will always ensure human subject protections and follow required safety protocols."

This environment of constant research and learning also makes CVN clinics good training sites for new clinicians. There is a chronic shortage of medical professionals with expertise in care of veterans. CVN is capitalizing on this by financing interns at their clinics from top-flight schools of social work like the University of Pennsylvania, Columbia, and USC.

Finances
Each clinic costs between $750,000 and $1.2 million to set up, and $2 million annually to serve 500 patients. When split among 25 clinics and research projects, even Cohen's $325 million gift will go fast. So built into CVN's startup plan for each clinic, and the network as a whole, is a pathway to long-term financial sustainability. At the network level, Cohen, Hassan, and the board of directors will recruit other donors to provide co-funding once the model has proven its merits. Hassan is also trying to negotiate reimbursement agreements with TRICARE (the military's health care program for active-duty servicemembers, their families, and retirees) and the V.A.'s new Veterans Choice program, which allows some veterans to seek

care from convenient medical providers when the local V.A. facility is over-burdened or too far away. If he can convince the bureaucracies to agree to even partial reimbursements this would allow the philanthropic dollars being spent on these veterans to go much farther.

Each new clinic is expected to quickly qualify itself for reimbursements from private health insurers. Each also raises some annual operating funds from their community, with guidance from CVN. Currently, the plan is to offset about $20 million of the total $45 million annual cost via third-party payments, philanthropy, and other funding.

> It's a misconception that traumatic stress disorder is an epidemic. Even among veterans who step into the Cohen mental-health clinics, only about 20 percent have those symptoms.

To give the network a strong spine, CVN allocates $2-3 million per year to maintain a strong back office that can provide all of the system services the programs need. It manages data processing, financial modeling, IT support, research coordination, event and media management, and marketing for each clinic. "Our partners see that they are now part of a powerful network," says Hassan. "This is especially important for the small community health clinics in our network. They're now able to communicate with some of the best clinicians and experts across the country. If they have an innovative idea, it has the potential of being realized because of the network's research capacity. It's a very special and unique opportunity to be a partner of the Cohen Veterans Network."

Amidst these efforts to efficiently control costs and diversify revenue streams, the Cohen Veterans Network is determined to avoid charging patients for the mental-health support they receive. As CVN board member Admiral Mike Mullen put it, "serving those who don't have other options" is a primary focus of the group.

Deepening the science

The more Steve Cohen learned about post-traumatic stress, and brain injuries, the more he came to believe that the surrounding science needed to be deepened and improved. In 2013, he began inviting top researchers to working breakfasts at his house on Saturdays and Sundays. The investigators made presentations on the state of knowledge in the field. They often highlighted the gaps that exist.

For example:

- Clinicians have no objective diagnostics to know whether someone actually has PTSD. Doctors must rely primarily on self-reported symptoms that are difficult to verify and separate from other mental conditions.
- Scientists lack a firm grasp on what type of individual is most susceptible to having his mental equilibrium disrupted by stressful events.
- They likewise lack systematic information about whether different types of stress produce different disorders.
- It is not known why certain patients respond to certain treatments, while others don't.
- The number of therapies that have any evidence proving they work is small, and there is little consensus or momentum in developing additional drugs, psychotherapies, or devices showing evidence of effectiveness.
- Stress disorders are too fuzzy, subjective, and risky to attract much pharmaceutical investment, and bureaucratic regulations that control experiments involving human subjects are so suffocating that very little other research or experimentation is taking place in this area.

After dozens of meetings and scores of conversations, Cohen recognized that one of the best ways he could contribute in this area would be to turbo-charge the scientific research. The aim would be to try to create the first definitive diagnostics, and make progress on life-changing remedies. "The treatments we have today fall short," he said in a 2016 speech.

The immediate motivation for this was for veterans, but brain injuries and stress disorders aren't just incurred in military work. They can afflict car-crash survivors, crime victims, athletes at all levels, firefighters and police officers, disaster survivors, and persons exposed to sexual or childhood trauma. The positive spillover effects of addressing this issue among veterans could be felt across society.

Cohen's 2013 donation to Charles Marmar's search for systematic bio-markers of PTSD was a large downpayment—$17 million—toward more systematic research on the health of veterans. Initially, the philanthropist planned to match this with additional grants to other university labs willing to launch similarly ambitious efforts. He soon concluded, however, that a better use of additional funds would be to pool existing health data to unlock overlooked correlations.

Major breakthroughs in understanding medical syndromes often emerge when many different data sets are aggregated, so patterns can be discerned. Historically, research efforts on brain injury and traumatic stress have been dispersed and relatively small-gauge, and limited by modest research samples that are disconnected from one another. Since brain science is a particularly mysterious and opaque branch of biology, with essential functions often controlled by complex interactions

> Cohen recognized that one of the best ways he could contribute in this area is to turbo-charge the scientific research.

between different centers, understanding the whole is often much more complicated than summing together the parts. But there has not been one clearinghouse that pulls together existing information for larger analysis. Even basic physical data like blood samples, DNA, behavioral statistics, body scans, and so forth have not been connected in one database. There are reasons for this (beyond the fact that mental health is not a glamorous or profitable academic field)—it is expensive, difficult work. And the crisscrossing incentives of government, academic, and industry research have not encouraged sharing of information.

The best mechanism for stitching together research in ways that yield practical patient diagnostics and therapies is often philanthropy. Charitable donors often build connections across research entities at universities, in government, and in the private sector, without becoming bound to any one of them in particular. Cohen needed to do for brain injuries and stress disorders what other philanthropists have done for autism, schizophrenia, Alzheimer's, and Parkinson's diseases—funnel research dollars to promising new approaches, raise awareness and support patients, and encourage investments in treatments.

Bringing clinics and labs together

In 2015, Cohen made a $30 million grant to an organization founded by Magali Haas, a physician scientist with 15 years of experience running clinical trials for Johnson & Johnson, turning it into an autonomous non-profit called Cohen Veterans Bioscience that is charged with incubating diagnostic tests and remedies for people who suffer from brain injury or traumatic stress. CVB's structure and funding allows it to dispense with many of the steps important to traditional university or industry research (personal recognition, patents, tenure publications, and so forth) and just focus on science that could help patients. It shares research samples and intellectual property with less concern about giving up funding or reputation to a competitor. Rather than conducting its own research with in-house scientists, CVB coordinates collaborative research across existing labs like the Broad Institute at MIT.

Magali Haas and Anthony Hassan have been asked to closely coordinate the work of their respective pieces of Steven Cohen's funding for veterans mental health. The clinical information and results coming out of network clinics will be intensively studied by the bioscience analysts. Eventually it is hoped that guidance will flow the other way. Cohen says he aims to "put breakthroughs to use in our clinics so veterans can benefit right away."

With five Cohen Veterans Network clinics open by the end of 2016, this vision is well underway. The new facilities in Philadelphia, San Antonio, Dallas, Los Angeles, and New York (some open less than a year) have already delivered care to more than 1,300 patients. Progress can be expected to accelerate dramatically over the next few years—as the $325 million that Steven Cohen has so far pledged to his effort to elevate mental health among veterans begins to produce effects.

Training the Trainers:
The Jonas Center fills our nursing pool

Donald Jonas served in the Marine Corps in the early 1950s. Then he began a career in retail sales that brought him great success. He ultimately founded three national chains selling housewares or department-store goods. He and his wife Barbara became quite wealthy—and quite philanthropic. They became active leaders with the Guggenheim Museum, the KIPP charter school network, the American Jewish Congress, the Horace Mann School, and Heifer International.

They also created a large art collection, which they intended to donate to the public when they passed away. But when the collection's value appreciated far beyond their expectations, the couple decided not to wait. They resolved to sell some of the most valuable pieces and then plow the proceeds into charitable work.

In 2004 they set up a donor-advised fund and gifted 15 paintings to it. These were then offered for sale at Christie's. The auction seeded the Jonas Family Fund with over $44 million.

The delighted family began to consider which causes they would most like to assist with the resulting funds. They considered medical research, mental health, and public education. Finally they settled on nursing, and eventually veterans as well.

There have been hundreds of thousands of unfilled nursing positions in the U.S. for years. By 2022, the American Association of Colleges of Nursing estimates, job openings in the field will top one million. Why so many jobs? The nation has too many nurses in some places, and not enough in a great many other locales. Our aging population is increasing demand for nurses. And many nurses are themselves reaching retirement age.

V.A. hospitals are particularly vulnerable to this trend. A 2015 Inspector General report ranked nurses as the second most critical staffing need in the V.A. health-care workforce, ahead of psychologists and physical therapists. Though it hired nearly 7,300 nurses in 2014, it lost over 4,500 that same year.

There is a bottleneck that limits the ability of the U.S. to overcome our nurse shortage: too few instructors. In 2014, 78,000 applicants were turned away from nursing schools in part because there weren't enough professors to go around. There are currently about 1,500 open faculty positions in nursing schools around the country. That is where the Jonas family decided to make its mark.

The Jonas Center

Within a year of their art auction, Donald and Barbara had established the Jonas Center for Nursing and Veterans Healthcare. Its basic thesis was this: if the first bottleneck in the nursing pipeline is a lack of qualified professors, trainers, and instructors, investments are needed to expand the number of individuals with doctorates and other teaching degrees in nursing. Scholarship support could encourage the next generation of instructors to learn the trade and fill areas of critical need.

Two years after creating the Jonas Center, a dedicated program was launched, with a $2.5 million commitment from the family, to train new leaders and scholars in nursing. Partnerships were established with leading nursing schools to create two-year $20,000 scholarships in support of doctoral candidates in nursing. A commitment of that size is sufficient to substantially improve degree-completion rates, without having to foot the recipient's entire schooling bill. Scholars are also offered leadership development, funding to attend the Jonas Center's annual nursing conference, and access to a strong alumni network.

Darlene Curley had worked as a registered nurse, taught in the field for decades, and built a hundred-person company of visiting nurses serving rural Maine, while also serving in the state's legislature. In 2009 she was hired to lead the Jonas Center, and charged with turning its promising regional scholarship for nursing instructors into a national effort. The center began expanding the number of partner institutions where it offered scholarships. It built a top-flight advisory board. And it brought in other donors to expand its efforts. By 2016, the program had funded 1,000 nurse faculty and clinical leaders in all 50 states.

Adding veterans to the mix

Around 2010, like many donors, Donald Jonas recognized some of the challenges new veterans were facing. He decided to do something about it. Rather than opening an entirely new grantmaking portfolio, his charity's board encouraged him to harness its existing expertise. The result was the Jonas Veterans Healthcare Program.

"In 2011 we reached out to 20 schools of nursing near military facilities," says Curley. "The University of San Diego was the first to respond, and by the next day we had an agreement. Only with private philanthropy is that sort of brisk action possible. Our first pilot in San Diego started with five nurses, and we grew from there."

The Jonas Center specifically sought out institutions that had relationships with local V.A. hospitals, so they could share discoveries and work together. That turned out to be difficult to achieve. The center approached the V.A. secretary, the "Joining Forces" initiative promoted by the White House as a way of linking government and philanthropy, the V.A. department of nursing, the V.A. research department, and the V.A. office of policy planning. Individuals within each bureaucracy saw the clear value of what the Jonas Center offered. But it took five years for the Jonas Center to secure a simple agreement that allows its scholars to share research with the V.A.

The Jonas Veterans Healthcare Program only accepts candidates who have experience with veterans, or are veterans themselves. It has recruited V.A. nurses looking to advance their careers. But it includes candidates working in a variety of medical settings. "Only a third of veterans get their care at the V.A.—everyone else is out in the community," notes Curley. "We are working to advance the knowledge and education of nurses who work in the V.A., but also those who are working with veterans all over the country."

> Each new nursing professor teaches 200 nurses a year—helping propel 5,000 additional nurses into the profession over a 25-year career.

The Jonas Center seeks out candidates with special research interests relevant to vets. "We've been very specific about the percentage we want to be studying poly-trauma, prosthetics, care coordination, brain injuries, traumatic stress, suicide prevention, aging, and other areas where there are clear percentages of veterans who have those diagnoses," states Curley. It also directly funds research in these kinds of areas. "I reached out to all nursing schools with a specialty in pain management and said 'we have funding for nurses working on pain focused on veterans.' I had ten schools get back to me in a week."

"Our next effort will be to target our scholarships geographically. We've been doing some mapping so that next time we recruit, I can say, 'Where is there need for more psych nurse practitioners? For more geriatric nurses?' And we'll go out and recruit at schools near those places of high need."

Rounding up partners

The Jonas Family Fund has so far invested $7 million in its effort to train nurses to serve veterans. It has also rounded up partners to put additional funds into the effort. These include the Ahmanson Foundation, Bob Woodruff Foundation, Milbank Foundation, May and Stanley Smith Charitable Trust, Ralph M. Parsons Foundation, Robert R. McCormick Foundation, and others.

As of 2016, the Jonas Center had supported 285 scholars at 80 universities via its program centered on vets. Already, some of these Jonas Scholars have moved into crucial roles in the military or veteran health systems. One, for instance, is the director of surgical services at a Navy hospital. Others work at research and clinical sites like the V.A. Polytrauma Clinic, the Defense and Veteran Brain Injury Center, the Walter Reed Medical Center, and the San Antonio Military Medical Center.

The Jonas family has committed to continuing its donations to nursing education through 2028, a substantial portion of which will remain focused on the particular needs of veterans. Its scholarships delivered through nursing schools proved to be an effective way to expand the nursing pipeline. The Jonas Center estimates that each nursing professor teaches 200 nurses per year—helping propel 5,000 nurses into the profession over a 25-year career. And significant numbers of these additional nurses are being strategically targeted by the funder into special fields of need—in addition to its special interest in veterans, the center has offered special support for nurses focused on mental health in Nevada, diabetes in West Virginia, and other niches recommended by its advisory board. Thus do the Jonas gifts bolster needed expertise as well as necessary numbers of professionals.

Making Vets a Focus:
The Weinberg Foundation extends its donor intent to a new field

For decades, the Weinberg Foundation has been known as a dedicated funder of programs that help vulnerable individuals and families. Its $100 million annual budget is focused on vulnerable older adults, job training, the homeless, early-childhood education, people with disabilities, and Jewish causes in the U.S. and abroad.

Harry Weinberg went to work soon after finishing sixth grade. He eventually built a real estate and transportation empire. With the proceeds, he and his wife Jeanette created a large foundation in 1959, based in his native Baltimore, to care for the poor and the vulnerable.

Weinberg left very specific guidelines about how his dollars were to be spent. The foundation would focus on the topics listed above, and target its giving whenever possible on the places where Harry had lived and succeeded in business—Maryland, northeast Pennsylvania, Hawaii, and Illinois. As a real-estate developer, Harry understood how a timely building could incubate many useful human activities, so he mandated that 50 percent of his foundation's grants should support capital projects. The other half of the foundation's annual spending would go to flexible funding that good charities can use to cover any of the expenses they face. Harry asked that his funding not go to universities or the arts. He respected those institutions but thought they had plenty of patrons, and that his donations should go to less glamorous causes. While others "are finding the cures for all the ills of the world, someone will be hungry, someone will be cold. That's our job," he stated.

Harry and Jeanette Weinberg wanted to promote human dignity and independence, mainstreaming into society those who are on the margins, and moving people to self-reliance. They didn't just fund the elderly generically, they aimed to help them age in their own homes and maintain agency in their lives. Weinberg's deep and long-running support for people with disabilities has emphasized helping them stand on their on feet. The foundation's education and job-training ventures aspire to enable people to provide for themselves.

Applying old ethics to a new field
In the late 1990s, the Weinberg Foundation made its first grant touching on military service—but through a back door: its longstanding donor commitments to Maryland and to Jews. A $1.5 million grant was given to help build a Jewish chapel and activity space at the United States Naval Academy in Annapolis. Over the next decade and a half, the foundation trickled about $6 million into additional grants that touched veterans in one way or another.

Some Weinberg grants went to prominent nonprofits that serve many populations, including veterans. Others went to organizations zeroed in on vets and servicemembers (like its grants to Fisher House, the organization that offers free housing for families of individuals recovering from injuries at military and veteran hospitals, and to Baltimore Station and MCVET, local homeless shelters and supportive housing programs focused on vets). Like many funders, Weinberg saw veterans as an increasingly important population, and it made grants as opportunities emerged.

Then foundation trustee Donn Weinberg attended a Philanthropy Roundtable conference where he heard a new take on what it meant to support veterans and persons with disabilities. West Point professor and Iraq war amputee Daniel Gade urged the donors in attendance to focus on what veterans can do, rather than what they cannot. Rather than assuming they are broken and need aid, philanthropists should treat veterans as a resource and help them make the most of their talents. (Gade's themes are featured in his "Setting the Scene" chapter in *Serving Those Who Served*.)

This message resonated with Donn Weinberg. "It's an approach that fosters self-support rather than dependence. We want to see veterans involved in society, not reliant on disability pay unless it's necessary. That is a better and more fulfilling life." Helping veterans become civilian successes would be a natural extension of Harry Weinberg's work.

> We want to see veterans self-supporting and involved in society, not dependent. That is a better and more fulfilling life.

Though the foundation was already dabbling in veterans' funding as described above, Donn Weinberg concluded its existing work was inadequate and too generalized. The fact "that The Philanthropy Roundtable had established a new program centered on veterans gave me the idea that we should have one too." The foundation could do a lot more good if it "dealt with veterans as a focus area, not a collateral matter, touching on them from time to time." It was also encouraging to know that wisdom and experience from other donors was being collected and made available for other funders to draw on, says Donn.

Program officer Kate Sorestad, who was in charge of Weinberg's general community-support portfolio, made a suggestion to the board of directors. She noted that "veterans hit every one of our portfolios—education, workforce development, disabilities, basic human needs." A dedicated funding pool would be a chance to add sophistication to the foundation's giving, and bridge its current hodge-podge of projects into something more methodical.

The trustees liked the logic, but asked why the foundation should get involved in an area that already had massive government investment. Wasn't the government taking care of this population? What difference would a million dollars a year from Weinberg make? Donn provided the answer: "the government has severe limitations because it is a rule-based bureaucracy, is not flexible, and doesn't have the incentives to make people more productive."

Trustees also wondered whether the foundation had the expertise necessary to evaluate proposals in this new field. How hard would it be to separate out promising ideas from ones that could be wasteful, counterproductive, or even fraudulent? Many of the nonprofits now serving veterans are recently formed, and still evolving.

The trustees decided these hurdles were no excuse to sit on the sidelines. The foundation would set careful funding guidelines and then experiment with providers and issue areas in a deliberate way, and thus gradually develop expertise and comfort that it could donate money effectively to meet the foundation's goals. In January, the trustees set aside $2 million per year for the new portfolio, and began defining a strategy.

Setting guidelines

"As a foundation, we always look to build self-sufficiency," explains Sorestad. So the foundation announced in 2016 that it would be interested in proposals for helping veterans succeed and stand on their own in three specific areas: Programs to speed veterans into the civilian workforce. Support for veterans with serious injuries, including health services, home rehabilitation, and community support. And efforts to overcome barriers that could block veterans from succeeding, like legal support, financial and other counseling, and so forth.

"We are too broad in our focus, but that's intentional at this early stage. These are places for us to start," says Sorestad. As experience accumulates, it is likely the foundation will narrow down on the most successful areas.

As with all other Weinberg grants, there is a preference for the Weinberg hometowns, but also a willingness to fund national programs that are excellent, a substantial allocation to capital projects, and more willingness to fund general-operating support than most foundations will offer. And like elsewhere, this veterans' program will honor Harry Weinberg's desire to avoid colleges, research, and art. The early veterans' grants have mostly been smaller than is typical for the foundation. This makes a lot more work for the foundation, but fits the experimental strategy which will seek exposure to a range of issues and service providers before narrowing things down for long-term grantmaking.

Sorestad was honest with herself and others about the challenges of starting a new effort from scratch. But she threw herself into the task with relish, and drew heavily on the expertise of others, including the program in veterans' philanthropy that The Philanthropy Roundtable had launched in 2012.

Sorestad formed an advisory committee (a mechanism she had also relied upon for a major library-funding initiative she had steered). She recruited ten impressive members from a wide variety of nonprofit, business, local government, and military backgrounds. They offered her broad knowledge and judgment, as well as very specific assistance with tasks like adapting the foundation's standard grant application so it would capture the information most relevant for serving veterans.

Every month, Sorestad sends her advisory-board members material from grant applicants for confidential review and feedback. "What I love about my advisory committee is that because they come from different sectors, topics areas, and philosophical perspectives, they sometimes give very different opinions. It's definitely not a 'yes' committee. I get some really good, honest answers." To these, Sorestad adds insights from regular conversations with other funders and charities tackling veterans' issues around the country.

"This way, I can take a range of responses to the trustees so it's not just me saying, 'well, it seems like a good fit.' I get confidential information and an insider's perspective on what we should be looking at." Organizations that get an initial thumbs-up from the trustees are invited to deliver a full proposal within two months.

The Weinberg Foundation is at the beginning of its activity in this area, and may fund some flops as well as successes. But it has thoughtfully added a new permanent portfolio to support veterans in a way that both maintains its original donor intent and positions the program to get better and better over time. "I'm excited and optimistic about the honing and strengthening of the portfolio that will come through future funding cycles," says Sorestad. "We'll tighten things up. But I'm glad we decided to just say, 'Go. Let's try it.'"

A Re-boot: Centering the USAA Foundation anew on military men and women

In 1922, a group of military officers in San Antonio, Texas, were having trouble qualifying for car insurance, so they formed their own member-owned company, the United Services Automobile Association, to provide coverage to other servicemembers like them. Eventually, rules were relaxed to serve many civilians as well. Today, USAA provides insurance, banking, investments, and financial advising to over 11 million individuals.

Eventually the firm established the USAA Foundation and USAA Educational Foundation as independent nonprofit arms. They were endowed by the company to make small charitable grants in the communities that hosted large corporate offices—first San Antonio, then Phoenix, Norfolk, Colorado Springs, and Tampa. Eventually they began to serve the public at large.

Paths to a brand-new giving strategy

In 2013, the long-time leader of the USAA Foundation retired and the company sought a successor. It was looking for someone who knew the company inside and out and could bring a fresh set of eyes to its allied charitable efforts. Enter Harriet Dominique. Her view of the foundation was that "this is a business we're running and our bottom line is social impact. Business changes with the times, and we must be no less disciplined." A broad review of the foundation's mission, and opportunities for the future, was launched.

The review suggested that for a national company, too much of its charitable giving was devoted to its San Antonio hometown, and that a new strategy for making gifts should accompany a more national focus. USAA's corporate philanthropy, it was proposed, should be grouped into two broad categories: continued local giving, and a signature cause. "We have a responsibility to take care of the backyard in which our employees live and serve," says Dominique. But USAA also wants to be "a leader on an important national cause. That's why you see two components of our strategy."

In each of its major communities, USAA would support charities devoted to three local priorities: Education, especially financial literacy and STEM-related learning. Disaster relief (both response and prevention). And family homelessness and hunger. These topics fit with USAA's expertise as an insurer and bank.

When it came to establishing a national-level signature cause, the foundation started with its company's original mission: boosting financial security in the military community. It spoke to more than 150 experts about the status and needs of our military population. Then it commissioned a survey of 2,500 members, customers, and employees to better understand what they would like to see from the company's corporate philanthropy. Finally, it studied the giving practices of 55 peer financial institutions and excellent corporate philanthropies.

As Dominique's deputy Justin Schmitt commented, "Identifying what *won't* be done is the first and hardest part." The foundation had to pass on lots of worthy causes as it sought the area where it could do the most good. Eventually it decided that its signature national charitable work would center on supporting wounded or killed servicemembers and their families, boosting the financial status of servicemembers, and helping veterans and military spouses get jobs.

Twice annually, the foundation seeks feedback on its direction from outside experts. "It's easy to hear all the pretty stuff," notes Dominique, but she asks these advisers "to tell us what's missing." A small working group of USAA employees was also created for each topic area to offer suggestions for giving. And a few company leaders started serving as a brain trust for Dominique and the foundation.

Ultimately, final decisions lay with the foundation officers. But with all of this expertise available, why not use it? Dominique says these various formal advisers "have such rich discussions and debates that it makes for a better product. And then they are ambassadors for our work across the business."

As part of this reorientation, USAA's executives and board committed to increasing the company's charitable giving from 0.4 percent of pre-tax income to 1.0 percent by 2018. USAA employees would also be offered two paid days per year where they could volunteer their services to charities, with special support for skills-based volunteering that would allow accountants, marketers, lawyers, and techies to donate their valuable talents to nonprofits. For the annual employee giving campaign, USAA would allow donations to any nonprofit, and match all contributions that fit the USAA Foundation strategy.

Before, few people "understood where USAA gives, why we give, and what drove our decisions," states Dominique. Now the company foundation takes care to communicate its decisions to everyone with a stake in the charitable enterprise—company employees, customers, and grantees, and to connect them with the clear new board-approved strategy. To give previous beneficiaries time to adjust to the foundation's new giving patterns, previous donations were wound down over a period of three years: Full funding in 2015. Two thirds of prior funding in 2016. Then one third in 2017. By 2018, all proposals will be assessed purely against the new strategy.

As it winnows down recipients and prepares to make fewer, but on average larger, gifts, USAA has divided beneficiaries into three groups. Signature gifts tend to extend over several years and exceed $250,000 in size, and require detailed reporting. Integrated gifts fall between

$100,000 and $250,000 and usually combine some sort of funding with employee volunteer opportunities. Philanthropic gifts are smaller donations to cover general operating costs of the recipient.

Adopting Veterans and Military Families

When it did its assessment of other corporate philanthropies, the USAA Foundation was surprised to see that no major peer had taken up the family caregivers who help some veterans with tasks of everyday life. The vast majority of these vets are elderly men cared for by their children. Some, however, are family members caring for severely ill or injured veterans from the most recent wars. These spouses, parents, or other family members sometimes experience a decline in health or financial stability as a result of the stresses of caregiving. The Elizabeth Dole Foundation, a nonprofit started by the former U.S. Senator, provides research and programming to support this population.

> It's easy to hear the pretty stuff, but we want our advisers to tell us what's missing.

Seeing an opportunity that fit its new strategy, the USAA Foundation funded the first-ever national caregiver registry. Previously, no one tracked these family members caring for veterans, or studied their challenges, or connected them with peers. Working with the Elizabeth Dole Foundation and the PsychArmor Institute, an online training platform focused on mental health, the USAA Foundation helped create a series of courses. These cover everything from navigating the V.A. bureaucracy to guidelines for intimacy after injury. In addition to its financial support, USAA provided quality control by having its working group (which includes military caregivers who work at the company) review every course and provide editorial feedback.

In another alliance, USAA supports the Tragedy Assistance Program for Survivors. This is a charity that provides resources and community for families of servicemembers who died in the line of duty. In addition to making it the beneficiary of employee fundraisers totaling $500,000, USAA has provided a $1 million gift to support the TAPS program that provides emergency financial assistance to families of the fallen. The

USAA Educational Foundation is also helping those families plan their financial futures, given their unique situations.

The Educational Foundation has remade itself as part of the re-boot of the main foundation. It has teamed up with the Association for Financial Counseling and Planning Education to create customized materials and training that financial counselors can use, for free, with military families. It developed video micro-lessons for its financial readiness program called "Command Your Cash," and built an app to help people track their spending and develop budgets. And it's begun working with Texas A&M, one of the nation's largest producers of commissioned military officers, to incorporate USAAEF financial training into ROTC requirements. In addition to helping those men and women handle their money, the hope is that this training will allow those officers to better advise those serving under them on ways to avoid financial pitfalls.

USAA is a philanthropic company. In 2015 it contributed more than $15 million to charity, and its employees contributed another $9 million, plus 452,000 volunteer hours. These totals will rise dramatically between now and 2018, given the firm's announced commitment to more than double the percentages it gives away. That financial flow, lashed to the careful new strategy USAA has put into place for steering and assessing its charitable gifts, makes it a donor to watch. And one of the places it most hopes to inspire and lead fellow corporate donors is in becoming more engaged with the needs of veterans and military families.

Rethinking Disability:
Donors launch an experiment that could spark seminal social reform

This chapter offers a slightly different perspective from those that precede it. It details the founding and setup of a donor collaborative we incubated here at The Philanthropy Roundtable. While it is early in its implementation, the project's development offers some lessons for funders aiming to tackle similarly large issues.

Our system for handling veterans with disabilities hasn't been properly modernized in a century. It is based on antiquated medical notions, and it enshrines completely outdated technological, legal, and social understandings of what people with disabilities are capable of. The current system, which was created soon after the World Wars, tallies up the number and severity of medical ailments logged for a servicemember, then condenses that into a single number that represents that person's disability rating. (This is often increased in subsequent years via appeals, which are unlimited.) Lifelong cash payments, plus eligibility for other benefits like lifelong health insurance for family members, then flow directly from that. The higher the rating, the higher the checks.

The nation now spends more on disability payments for veterans than it does on all of their physical and mental health care, or the rich G.I. Bill benefits to support their further education, or the entirety of its programs to help any veteran buy a house. In 2016, the V.A. mailed out disability-compensation checks totaling more than $68 billion. That's *three and a half times* as much (after adjusting for inflation) as we spent as recently as 2000. In that same short period, the percentage of U.S. veterans who are categorized as disabled has more than *doubled*. And the number of veterans claiming the very highest levels of disability (rated 70-100 percent) more than *tripled*. About half of all war-on-terror veterans are now applying for lifelong disability benefits.

These funds do not help people recover. They are not for physical therapy, or counseling, or devices to assist them at work, or training that will allow them to shift to a new occupation where their disability isn't an obstacle. This cash just says "Sit down. No need to get better. We don't imagine you being independent, or supporting yourself." These non-rehabilitative cash payments send the implicit message that the recipient is unfixable—delivered with no expectation or encouragement that he or she, no matter how young, will heal and become self-reliant. That's why veterans on disability compensation (studies show) respond to treatment and recover at much lower rates than people not receiving checks. Rather than getting better, the much more common pattern for veterans on disability is to steadily *climb up* to higher and higher ratings, less and less social and occupational activity, and more isolation and unhappiness.

Veterans with higher disability ratings are much more likely to drop out of the workforce—not because of functional limitations, but because of the economic incentives these checks impose. Then they end up in a precarious position: disability benefits are enough to dissuade many recipients from getting healing therapy and building a career, but they aren't enough to support a family in the long run.

This is a badly broken system. It is begging for a creative reimagining.

From problem to plan

In 2012, The Philanthropy Roundtable launched a program advising donors interested in veterans' causes. Karl Zinsmeister, who previously led veterans' policy at the White House and dealt intimately with the veterans' disability system while overseeing the Dole-Shalala Commission, provided guidance to the program and hired me (the author of this book) to run it. He also introduced me to a former member of his policy staff—Daniel Gade, an Iraq-war combat veteran and amputee who had

> The nation now spends more on disability payments for veterans than it does on all of their physical and mental health care, or the rich G.I. bill benefits, or the entirety of its programs to help any veteran buy a house.

gone on to earn a Ph.D. in social policy, and a position teaching at West Point. The three of us wondered whether private philanthropy could play a constructive role by funding a careful pilot program to demonstrate that there are better ways to treat veterans with disabilities. Together, we formulated a plan that would provide charitable funding to design and run a voluntary test of new supports, one that wouldn't require participants to give up their current benefits. It would invest in veterans with disabilities on the front end of their transition, support them in pursuing improved health and steady work, and reward them for success.

We presented our idea at a meeting of philanthropists in late 2013 and received strong interest. The Anschutz Foundation, Milbank Foundation, and Daniels Fund quickly stepped up to provide the initial funding to develop the idea. Carl Helstrom, director of the Milbank Foundation, describes his reaction: "We are a small foundation, and always asking how we can be most helpful with our limited funds. This was a classic pilot-project scenario where you need someone to jump in first, show other donors that you think it's promising and valuable, and give the creators enough resources so they can demonstrate whether their idea really works. It was a calculated risk, but it was one we thought worth taking, and very congruent with our mission of helping Americans overcome disabilities."

That kicked off a process of developing the idea into a focused business plan. We studied examples of other disability systems around the world that had been modernized in recent years. We took inspiration from U.S. programs that reward work, like the Earned Income Tax Credit. We drew lessons from the rising tide of philanthropic programs that are now helping economic strugglers hold jobs. We met with former V.A. secretaries, policy experts, and high-ranking military personnel for advice. We sought input from leading scholars like David Autor at MIT, Mark Duggan at Stanford, Rich McNally at Harvard, Sally Satel at AEI, and Chris Frueh at the Baylor College of Medicine.

Most important, we took their ideas to individuals in the process of transitioning out of military service and veterans with disabilities. Gade led the work running surveys and focus groups to better understand what these men and women feared, aspired to, and needed most to make successful jumps into civilian success. This research found deep dissatisfaction with the current disability system for vets, and a powerful hunger for alternatives.

The three of us designed a program that would test the effectiveness of different combinations of supports side by side. There would be flexible funds for training or equipment that would position individuals to garner attractive jobs. There would be wage bonuses to reward early transitions to work. There would be intensive mentoring, peer support, and high expectations.

The goal of all this would be crystal clear to participants—independence. Indeed, we chose that as the name of the initiative: The Independence Project. By the fall of 2014 we had a detailed 60-page business proposal, including a plan for tracking outcomes and a basic budget. The Anschutz Foundation became the pioneer funder with a $1 million grant that transformed the effort from fresh idea to actual undertaking. The Milbank Foundation re-upped its commitment, and the Wilf Family Foundations signed on too.

Big funding to hone the project
After earning a fortune making bold, research-intensive investments in energy, investor John Arnold and his wife Laura set up a foundation to

take on some of the nation's most complex and overlooked technical problems, with a special emphasis on producing data that proves the viability of new solutions. The foremost push of the foundation is for "evidence-based policymaking." Josh McGee, a trained economist, runs much of the foundation's work in this area. For many donors, evaluation is an afterthought, but the Arnold Foundation considers it a core function. It hopes that this will eventually become a routine part of all philanthropy and public policy aimed at influencing social behavior.

McGee explains the value of such investments:

> I liken it to the field of medicine, which was in the dark ages not so long ago. In George Washington's day we thought bloodletting was an appropriate treatment for a whole host of ailments, because nothing was actually tested out methodically. Eventually we started using the scientific method to compare one course of action to another—whether various treatments made an improvement or not. That transformed medicine. But we were never that rigorous when it came to testing human behavior. In social services and government policy, we're still in the guesswork phase.

In 2014, Arnold Foundation president Denis Calabrese learned about the Independence Project and asked McGee to take a look. At first inspection, he says, "it fit our interest in evidence-based policies, and testing new ideas to figure out better ways of solving hard social problems." But the Arnold Foundation is an extremely picky grantor. "We ask, 'Is this an intervention with a solid probability of success? Is it new, or has this subject already been explored?' We care a lot about the evidence any project will produce, and whether the charitable intervention includes hard tests of its own effectiveness," notes McGee.

He asked for exact details of the various tools the Independence Project would use with participants. Is there any prior precedent for the flexible training funds you're proposing? Where has career coaching worked in the past to help people get jobs? No one had ever tried any of these supports with American veterans, so analogies from other fields had to be explored: Field tests with dislocated workers, welfare families, civilians with disabilities, veterans in other countries, and so forth.

The Arnold Foundation agreed that veterans are a worthy population to assist. It also believed that any lessons about better ways of doing disability compensation among veterans would have valuable implications for the larger population of Americans stuck on disability. It wanted in. But it wanted a strong evaluation process so no opponent could shrug off results as an "anomaly," or "not reproducible."

After several rounds of rigorous refinement, the Arnold Foundation board approved the plan. And in the summer of 2015, they committed $4.1 million of support. The Independence Project was no longer pie in the sky.

A wide range of donors find common cause

Doing the experiment at this depth and quality was going to require more than $10 million. With a rich design now in hand, we approached other funders. A dozen eventually signed on.

All had their own motivations and particular interests—which strengthened the project. The Anschutz Foundation, the first major donor to commit, wanted to see veterans thrive over the long run. Fellow Coloradans at the Daniels Fund, whose patron had been formed by military service before he went into business, followed a key motto of Bill Daniels: "Value people for what they can do, not for what they can't." The Morgridge Family Foundation invested as part of its founder's commitment to promoting self-sufficiency. The Lynde and Harry Bradley Foundation saw triple potential in the project: a chance to help patriotic veterans, to improve government effectiveness, and to avoid a fiscal drain of billions of taxpayer dollars. The Weinberg Foundation found many of its cherished interests embedded in the project: disability issues, workforce development, and veterans. And the Kovner Foundation made the project the core of its new venture into supporting veterans.

Asked about her motivation to join, Kovner Foundation co-chair Suzie Kovner says, "I believe that work is what contributes to one's self-esteem, sense of community and capabilities. If some veterans, who are among our bravest and most capable citizens, are being encouraged to languish on disability benefits, I wondered if there wasn't a better way to get them incentivized, to get them back into the workforce, and enable them to live more fulfilling lives."

For the Independence Project's largest donor—the Diana Davis Spencer Foundation—the project aligned with several crucial priorities. The foundation is a dedicated supporter of charities that aid military families. It has longstanding interests in improving the quality of public policies. And perhaps the highest priority for the foundation is national security. Ensuring that veterans with disabilities transition successfully into the workforce both strengthens the U.S. economy and extends the viability of our all-volunteer military force.

And all the donors cherished high hopes that the lessons of the Independence Project could be broadly applicable to all individuals, and help civilians with disabilities thrive as well.

Building an all-star team

The Philanthropy Roundtable developed and incubated the Independence Project. But the Roundtable is not an operating philanthropy. A great charitable service provider was needed to implement the program. Top researchers would be required to handle the evaluation.

The first option considered was to launch an entirely new nonprofit. But that would require legal incorporation, staffing, and startup energy. Most importantly, a new organization would lack deep trial-and-error experience at delivering high-quality services. Rather than reinvent the wheel, we went looking for the very best nonprofits working with people with disabilities and with veterans. We had several criteria:

- *Mission alignment.* The organization needed to share the underlying philosophy of the project that veterans should be invested in, not given incentives to sit on the sidelines.
- *Experience at delivering similar services.* Some components of the Independence Project had never been applied to vets, but others were drawn from the best practices of existing nonprofits. The Independence Project hoped to find a partner already very experienced and successful in connecting veterans to jobs.
- *Capacity for growth.* Any organization taking on the initiative would need to be able to manage a large budget, staff, and complex programs at a high level of quality, without getting overwhelmed.
- *Infrastructure for collecting data.* Understanding how participants are doing, and later being able to prove what factors allow veterans with disabilities to thrive, are crucial to this project's ultimate success. So the executing partner had to be savvy and capable at collecting data.

Dozens of potential organizations were assessed. We relied heavily on guidance from funders (like Dan Goldenberg at the Call of Duty Endowment) who were already supporting organizations in the running. After months of searching, Hire Heroes USA proved to be an ideal partner for the job. A strong theme of self-reliance underlies all of the organization's programming. Several elements of the Independence Project, like intensive job coaching, are already part of its standard procedures. The organization has superb leadership, and a proven ability to recruit and train good staff. Hire Heroes USA was also already a sophisticated collector and user of data, as it methodically studies the impact of its own programs and how they can be improved. Finally, the group had demonstrated many times that it knew how to open new ventures and expand programming without sacrificing quality. HHUSA brought on a director who would be responsible for executing the program—Ross Dickman, who was just leaving the Army after 12 years as a combat veteran, helicopter pilot, and trainer of cadets at West Point.

> "This is probably something that could only be funded by private philanthropy," says Frueh.

HHUSA and the program's new director brought their on-the-ground experience in service delivery to bear, turning the paper plan into a concrete program. They incorporated their already-successful practices into the Independence Project, developed procedures for new components, and hired and trained an execution team.

We searched simultaneously for external evaluators who could carry out rigorous tests of the program and provide an independent assessment of its impact. Many experts were excited by the Independence Project; several said its use of incentives and aid and testing was unlike any effort they had seen. "This is probably something that could only be funded by private philanthropy," says Frueh.

Finding the right evaluator was tricky—top-rated private firms charge exorbitant fees, while individual academics rarely have the resources required by this ambitious experiment. It was also a challenge to balance getting the program operating quickly and efficiently with the pace and procedure of academic evaluation. So the Independence Project first launched a smaller pilot version of the program so that procedures can be tested and adjusted before heavy investments are made in gold-standard evaluation.

Governance of an unusual donor collaborative

With a dozen donors involved in the Independence Project, each with different giving priorities and levels of funding, we had to give considerable thought to a governing structure that could fairly oversee the project as it developed over a multi-year period, and make course corrections if needed. We wanted to make sure that all donors to this pioneering project would remain informed, without demanding too much of our oversight.

Instead of having many separate relationships between the 12 funders and the program operators and researchers, most grants were pooled in a special fund opened at the Communities Foundation of Texas. Contributions are safely parked there for distribution as pre-agreed milestones are reached by the project.

As incubator of the project, The Philanthropy Roundtable took responsibility for releasing payments and reporting progress back to all donors. This allows the grantees to focus tightly on running a successful project. To keep donor intent at the fore, a small oversight committee with special expertise was created to release grants and make any course corrections. As member Suzie Kovner explains, "the oversight committee keeps me closer to the project and allows me to understand the unexpected challenges of conducting such an ambitious study. Luckily this means we can adapt and change as we learn what we are doing right and what we might need to improve."

First put into operation in early 2017, the Independence Project is still in its infancy. But it serves as a model for major donor collaborations that marshal charitable funds, philanthropic expertise, and nonprofit management to address America's biggest and most complex social problems. Donors to causes of all sorts will want to study this ambitious and entrepreneurial effort closely for new lessons on the expanding capacities of American philanthropy.

LESSONS AND OPPORTUNITIES

Lessons from the field

Here are simple summaries of some of the key things you can learn from today's best giving for vets—as presented in detail in the 12 case studies you've just read.

Call of Duty Endowment

CODE ignores name brands and good intentions and instead focuses its money in a disciplined way on charities that can demonstrate concrete, measurable returns. The endowment makes just one kind of grant—growth funding, solely for nonprofits that help veterans find work—which makes assessing and comparing nonprofits much more manageable. Every grantee passes a two-part audit examining organizational strength, financial stability, program delivery, and impact before qualifying to apply for a large grant. Recognizing that every nonprofit is different, CODE is still able to settle on a common group of outcome measures: number of veterans placed, quality of work (salary and full/part time status), and cost of placement.

Schultz Family Foundation

The Schultz Family Foundation built a single end-to-end employment pipeline that can carry veterans to many different types of industries and employers. Schultz and its nonprofit partners are able to connect individuals to training programs for high-demand careers starting months before they leave the service, thanks to some complicated coordination with partners in the Defense Department. Their program starts from the needs of real employers with open jobs, and reverse engineers training programs that give future vets and military spouses marketable skills.

Kohlberg and Kisco Foundations

The Kohlberg and Kisco Foundations boosted college education of veterans by mixing direct services with policy efforts. Mr. Kohlberg gave out hundreds of scholarships to veterans all around the country, then helped recipients tell their stories to legislators who had the power to create a new G.I. Bill as useful to veterans as the one Kohlberg himself had used to prepare for his business career. Today's Post-9/11 G.I. Bill owes its existence in no small part to these efforts. Kohlberg's more recent work combines direct services with research and policy efforts to make sure that schools are serving student veterans well.

Ahmanson Foundation

Stick with what you know and who you trust—it can be a great way to move into a new philanthropic field with relatively little risk. Bill Ahmanson had decades-long funding relationships with two dozen private colleges and universities in Southern California, where he had funded everything from scholarships to science centers. He knew higher education could launch former servicemembers into successful civilian lives, so he gave each of his schools a recurring grant and a challenge to find ways to attract veterans to their campus. He gave them wide latitude to use the funding as they saw fit, but required annual reports on how they improved their capacities to "recruit, retain, and educate" veterans. This high level of trust opened schools up to experimentation and new programming.

J. A. and Kathryn Albertson Foundation

Philanthropy in a rural state has advantages and disadvantages—there aren't as many top-performing nonprofits, but there is great potential to have a clear impact. The Idaho-based Albertson Foundation has decades of experience navigating those waters and brought its knowledge to bear when it decided to go to work on veterans' issues in the state. Not finding organizations in Idaho that fit its needs, the foundation recruited well-established national providers to stand up local chapters and offices. Albertson provided substantial management, advertising, and institutional support beyond funding to help the imported service providers adjust their work to Idaho's needs and nature.

Heinz Endowments

The Heinz Endowments recognized early in the game that helping veterans succeed in civilian life would not only boost a worthy population, but also benefit the wider population in any community where veterans were helped to succeed. Heinz invested in a needs-assessment to understand what would most benefit Pennsylvania veterans, and what gaps needed bridging. It found too much existing focus on crisis management, so it planted its flag on prevention of problems and programs to make veterans productive citizens. Along with its portfolio of charities specializing in empowering individuals, it invested in a formal referral system to smoothly connect vets to different charities for varying needs.

Marcus Foundation

Bernie Marcus has made an indelible mark on the lives of the relatively small number of catastrophically injured veterans—to whom he has committed massive resources so they can have a measure of independent living. For those who need complex concussion care, he is providing free, world-class clinics outside of the V.A. bureaucracy. And for the large majority of veterans who transition into civilian life with simpler yearnings for continued purpose and camaraderie, he's funded a portfolio of organizations that extend esprit de corps into life after the military.

Cohen Veterans Network

The needs of veterans and their families for periodic help with mental health are not dramatically different from civilian families—many Americans wrestle at times with depression, child development issues, anger management, stress disorders. When Steve Cohen decided he wanted to support a provider of excellent assistance with these challenges he couldn't find an impressive network. So he built a team to launch one. The Cohen Veterans Network pinpoints areas of high need around the country, then works with local partners to stand up a high-quality clinic open to veterans, military personnel, and their families. Cohen simultaneously funded a separate research initiative that will use experience from the clinics to advance understanding and treatment of syndromes like traumatic stress disorders.

Jonas Family Fund

The Jonas family put its money on long-term real-world effectiveness rather than sentimental, photogenic programs. They asked what the biggest practical barriers to improved health care are for vets, and got an unglamorous but extremely concrete answer: there aren't enough nurses with expertise in the area. With this discovery in hand, they stepped even further in an unglamorous direction, up the training pipeline. If you want more, better-trained nurses, you have to have more good nursing professors who know something about vets. The family began to supply stimulative funding that is spurring the instruction of tens of thousands of nurses, and improving the quality of research on the intersection between nursing and the medical needs of former servicemembers.

Harry and Jeanette Weinberg Foundation

Getting into any new field of philanthropy always poses risk—how do you pick the right priorities, find good operators, and review your own work? The Harry and Jeanette Weinberg Foundation navigated this after realizing it was already backing work with veterans through other grants, and that it could create a freestanding vets emphasis by building on those existing grant streams and areas of expertise. So it stuck close to topics where it already had experience—disability, health, job training. It also clung tightly to its mission and charter, for instance, by favoring capital projects and general operating expenses, and not giving to higher education (priorities that came from its founders). It recruited an expert advisory committee, and started off with small grants broadly distributed, allowing it to gradually learn which providers respond best.

USAA Foundation

USAA triangulated three factors: What veterans and military families (upon whom their original business was founded) need. What their foundation is expert at providing. And what other corporate funders weren't addressing. Consultants, employee surveys, and peer comparisons were then employed to pick precise focus areas: military caregivers, financial preparedness of veterans, and jobs for vets and military spouses. The foundation then adjusted all of its operations—from its technology backbone, to its advisory groups, to the employee matching-gift campaign—to serve the new strategy.

Independence Project

The Independence Project is an example of the way intermediaries can organize donor collaborations that are big and savvy enough to attack deep, complex problems. This effort is using private philanthropy to experiment with dramatically new approaches to veterans enmeshed in the V.A. disability program, which discourages healing, self-improvement, independent activity, and work. It is reimagining ways that an outdated but entrenched program could be reformed so injured vets are able to rehabilitate themselves and become proud, self-reliant citizens.

Opportunities for donors

Now it's your turn. We hope that the sterling givers profiled in this book inspire you to make your own mark on the field. To start you off, we've listed below some ripe opportunities. Excitingly, many of these opportunities are already being pioneered by donors eager to partner with additional funders and expand good work. In other instances, there are chances for philanthropists to open new doors and originate important services for the first time.

Employment
- Expand the nonprofits identified by the Call of Duty Endowment as being most effective at getting veterans into jobs. A list of charities awarded its Seal of Distinction can be found at CallOfDutyEndowment.org. Some concentrate on particular regions; many serve veterans all around the country. You could support ongoing operations, bring the employment supports to a new place, or work with special sub groups like Reservists or candidates for engineering and tech jobs.
- Fund programs that help military spouses find work. Some organizations that support veteran employment, like Hire Heroes USA and Corporate America Supports You, also serve military spouses. Others, like Blue Star Families, focus specifically on military spouses.
- Fund a nationally representative study of the employment situation of veterans. Current government survey methods use weak definitions of employment, don't capture large enough samples to be meaningful, and don't capture hard-to-define problems like underemployment.
- Support existing efforts to begin training servicemembers for high-demand careers just before they leave the military. The Schultz Family Foundation's Onward to Opportunity program has already organized pathways, found training and job-search

providers, organized employer partners, and gotten difficult government approvals.

- Support charities that train veterans to start and run businesses, like Syracuse University's Entrepreneurship Bootcamp for Veterans, or peer learning environments and incubation spaces for veteran entrepreneurs like those provided by the Robert McCormick-funded Bunker Labs.
- Contribute to programs that match veterans and servicemembers with civilian career mentors who help them prepare for the labor market, like American Corporate Partners.
- Fund advocacy and programs that improve the translation of military certifications to civilian career fields, so that veterans can get recognition of the skills they have built up during their service. The Kresge Foundation has supported work along these lines through the Council for Adult and Experiential Learning.
- Support rigorous evaluation of promising employment programs. Many of the most exciting ones serving veterans still lack gold-standard evidence.
- Fund rigorous evaluations of public programs serving veterans—approximately 90 percent of all government programs have never been rigorously evaluated to determine effectiveness. Philanthropies like the Laura and John Arnold Foundation have invested heavily in measuring whether government programs are accomplishing what they set out to do.
- Support advocacy work to remove perverse incentives to employment built into many benefits for veterans, like disability compensation. This is a problem that plagues safety-net programs generally in America, but it is especially tragic when very young, public-spirited, abnormally experienced and talented veterans are sidelined by poorly designed entitlements.
- Support programs explicitly dedicated to moving veterans from dependence on government programs to self-reliance, meaningful careers, and community engagement.

Education

- Underwrite advisory counseling for veterans (preferably before they even leave military service) to improve their understanding of opportunities in higher education before they use their benefits, commit to schools, accumulate debt, and enter career paths that may not be optimal.

- Fund high-quality universities to expand their outreach to veterans and adjust their application processes for these non-traditional students.
- Fund a private university to expand the number of Yellow Ribbon slots (scholarships that cover the difference between G.I. Bill funding and private-school tuition) that it offers veterans. Because the V.A. matches any dollars universities invest, your money will be doubled.
- Fund academic bootcamps where veterans headed to college can refresh the skills they will need to succeed and graduate—for most it will have been years since stepping foot in a traditional classroom. Individual schools could provide this as a pre-orientation program. National organizations like the Warrior Scholar Project could expand the services they deliver to more students.
- Sponsor on-campus groups that provide veterans with peer support through the national chapter-based Student Veterans of America.
- Expand evidence-based programs shown to help student veterans navigate the challenges of college life and improve student retention rates, like the Bristol Myers-Squibb Foundation-funded Peer Advisors for Veteran Education.
- Support research into factors that promote student veteran success, as the Kisco Foundation is doing with community colleges around the country.
- Help high-performing employment organizations connect with student veterans as they approach graduation and find suitable careers.
- For student veterans whose G.I. Bill has been used up and who still have one or two semesters of schooling left to complete, create a revolving interest-free student-loan fund, or one in which payments represent a set percentage of income. You'll help bridge a funding gap without sinking veterans into unpayable debt, and the revolving nature of the fund will allow many veterans to benefit in the long run.
- Invest in efforts that help veterans get college credit for study, skills, and certifications they earned in the military. Forcing students to retake courses they mastered in the military is a waste of veteran

time and taxpayer dollars. Some funders like the Ahmanson Foundation and the Albertson Foundation have already supported this on a school-by-school basis. Others, like the Lumina Foundation, have taken a broader approach, funding the Midwestern Higher Education Compact to set guidelines which member schools follow, through the Multi-State Collaborative on Military Credit.

Physical and Mental Health

- For the catastrophically injured, fund surgeries that the DoD and V.A. will not cover or cannot provide in areas like facial, limb, and genital reconstruction. UCLA's Operation Mend has been offering plastic surgery and other reconstructive services to veterans for years now thanks to the support of generous donors like Ron Katz and David Gelbaum.
- Expand high-quality mental-health clinics that provide free, culturally competent care to veterans and military families in communities around the country, focusing on a range of adjustment-related conditions. Steve Cohen has already put cash on the barrelhead to organize a network of these clinics, pay for their launch, and conduct quality assurance. Contributing to the Cohen Veterans Network will leverage the substantial investment already made.
- Support intensive diagnostics and treatment for veterans who suffer long-term symptoms of concussion and brain injury. The Marcus Foundation has taken a lead role in organizing and vetting top-shelf clinics around the country like the SHARE Military Initiative at Shepherd Center. Help to expand this network of veteran concussion clinics.
- Help to stock the pool of healing talent serving veterans and military families by sponsoring medical, psychological, and social-work programs teaching about this population. The Jonas Fund has supported veteran-focused researchers to become nursing professors to expand competence among nurses; the University of Southern California School of Social Work has a focus on vets; and the Cohen Veterans Network trains young clinicians.
- Support research into the effectiveness and cost of non-traditional approaches to pain management and mental-health conditions. Many well-intentioned programs

exist, but few have enough evidence for veterans and their doctors to know what works.

- Support research and treatment of prescription-drug abuse in the veteran population. Although up-to-date research is limited, veterans today are likely facing the same problem with opioid addiction as Americans more broadly.
- Press for policy changes that would make it easier for community clinics and other health-care providers outside the V.A. apparatus to receive reimbursements for serving V.A.-eligible patients.

Family

- Family caregivers who spend significant time helping injured servicemembers perform the functions of daily life are often overlooked. Bolster organizations like the Elizabeth Dole Foundation, which raises funds to support research and services to aid relatives and friends who provide crucial care to injured veterans.
- Underwrite programs that help military families reconnect after deployments or other strains of military life. The Marcus Foundation and others have invested heavily in Boulder Crest, a retreat program that offers veterans and military families a chance to communicate and recharge.
- Fund research on ways to enhance the life quality of military families, such as is run every year by Blue Star Families. In addition to alleviating pressures on this population, it strengthens national security when servicemembers don't have to choose between family success and their military career.
- Support programs that help military spouses find work—their constant moving makes it particularly hard for them to locate and hold jobs and advance in their careers.
- Help charitable efforts, like the Tragedy Assistance Program for Survivors, that comfort Gold Star Families who have lost loved ones in military service.

Community

- Support organizations that promote healthy social activities for veterans, and mix them with community peers, leaders, and mentors. Team Red, White, and Blue provides very popular athletic outings through chapters all around the country—with many positive effects on physical and psychological health, community spirit, peer networking, family life, and social integration.

- Engage veterans in civilian service through organizations like The Mission Continues, Team Rubicon, or The 6th Branch. These serve community needs at the same time that they build purpose, camaraderie, and connection among veterans.
- If you aren't sure what the biggest needs of veterans in your area are, conduct a thorough needs assessment. Organizations like the Center for a New American Security, RAND, and the University of Southern California's Center for Innovation and Research on Veterans & Military Families all have experience running these.

Housing, Legal, and Financial

- Contribute to the building of adaptive smart-homes for the most catastrophically injured veterans. The numbers are not overwhelming—it is possible in the next five years to provide every catastrophically injured veteran with a home that allows independent living. Philanthropic leaders like the Marcus Foundation have already identified partners that get the job done quickly and efficiently.
- Support legal clinics that help veterans with routine civil legal problems like divorce, child support, landlord disputes, business licensing, financial liens, and so forth that can interfere with work, family life, and peace of mind. The Bristol Myers-Squibb Foundation-funded Connecticut Veterans Legal Center has been a national leader here.
- Expand opportunities for veterans in pre-trial diversionary programs (most commonly in the form of Veteran Treatment Courts).
- If you provide emergency financial assistance, structure it as an interest-free loan, and pair the funding with financial coaching to help make sure veterans and military families don't fall into the same money traps again.

Other

- Support a fellowship in journalism to report on veterans from the perspective that they are civic assets, not victims.
- Support longitudinal research on the particular identities, strengths, and needs of veterans who volunteered for service in

the post-9/11 era. They are different in important ways from previous generations of veterans. Nonprofits like the Henry Jackson Foundation and its Veterans Metrics Initiative can be helpful in pulling together factual information needed for customizing nonprofit work to be as effective as possible among a particular population.

VITAL
STATISTICS

Population

A total of 2.7 million servicemembers have served in the terror war sparked by the 9/11 attacks. Each year now about a third of a million individuals leave military service and become veterans. At present, terror-war vets make up 22 percent of all veterans. That will rise to 42 percent by 2030.

Current armed forces	2,152,164
Active duty	1,330,660
Reserve / National Guard	821,504

Deployments during terror war	
Servicemembers who were deployed at least once	2,726,102
Active duty	1,964,777
National Guard and Reserve	691,000

Veterans		
Individuals leaving military service in latest year (2015)		314,171
Veterans by era served—today, and 2030 projection[1]		
	2016	2030
Terror war	4,633,481	7,358,833
Gulf war	4,482,618	4,340,291
Vietnam	6,953,004	4,098,108
Korea	1,592,188	142,639
World War II	695,637	29,757
Total	21,368,156	17,421,211

1. Approximation due to some serving in multiple eras.

Sources: Defense Manpower Data Center (2017); Defense Manpower Data Center Deployment File (2015); Department of Defense "2015 Demographics: Profile of the military community"; Department of Veterans Affairs Vet Pop Model

Jobs

Of the 4.6 million men and women who served during the war on terror and are now out of the military, 19 percent are not in the labor force—they are in school, raising children, living on disability payments, or retired. Of those who are *in the labor force, 6 percent are unemployed. Spouses of members of the military, who must deal with moves and deployments, face special challenges getting jobs.[1]*

Unemployment rate		
	Veterans	Civilians
Men age 25-35	7%	5%
Women age 25-35	7%	6%
Men age 35-44	4%	4%
Women age 35-44	6%	4%

Labor force dropout rate		
	Terror-war veterans	Civilians
Men age 25-35	14%	11%
Women age 25-35	30%	27%
Men age 35-44	13%	9%
Women age 35-44	26%	26%

1. The average time spouses spend looking for work after each military-required move is five months.

Sources: Bureau of Labor Statistics "Household Data Annual Averages, Employment Status of persons 18 and over by veteran status, age, and sex" (2015); DoD Defense Manpower Data Center "Active Duty Spouses and Active Duty Members; Spouse Employment, Satisfaction, Financial Health, Relationships, and Deployments" (2015)

Education

There is a common misperception that many of the Americans who volunteer for military service do so because they lack skills to make it in the civilian economy. Actually, the young people who serve today exceed national norms, on average, in education and intelligence, health, and character qualities. On the whole, it is most accurate to think of people who have served in the military as a national asset, rather than a problematic population.

Recruit quality		
	Enlisted (officers excluded)	Civilians of the same age
Scored above average on aptitude tests	76%	50%
Have a high school degree	98%	87%

Educational attainment				
	Servicemembers	All veterans	Terror-war vets	Civilians 25+
No high school diploma	1%	7%	~0%	14%
High school or some college	77%	66%	65%	56%
Bachelor's degree or higher	22%	28%	34%	31%

Main specialties the military trains enlisted for	
Electrical	20%
Infantry, weapons, etc.	16%
Administration	13%
Supply	11%
Communications	10%
Electronics	9%
Medical	8%
Craftsman	3%

Sources: DoD "Population representation in the Military Services" (2014); V.A. "Veterans Economic Communities Pilot: 2016 Program Report"; DoD " 2015 Demographics: Profile of the Military Community"

Physical Injuries

Nearly all Americans agree that our society should pull out all the stops to heal and rehabilitate men and women injured during military service. Fortunately, compared to the millions who served in Iraq or Afghanistan, the number seriously hurt is much smaller than generally imagined.

Deaths during terror-war deployments	6,880
Wounded in action	52,482
Wounds serious enough to result in evacuation from theater	~15,000

	Casualty rate (wounded or killed)	Percentage of casualties wounded rather than killed	Percentage of veterans receiving (to date) disability compensation[1]
World War I	7%	64%	
World War II	7%	62%	11%
Korea	2%	74%	N.A.
Vietnam	4%	84%	16%
Gulf war	~0%	55%	21%
Terror war	1%	88%	33%

Major injuries during War on Terror	
Amputations	1,645
Serious burns	991
Genital injuries	1,387

Top disabilities claimed by veterans of War on Terror	
Ringing ears	434,094
Knee injury	316,792
Back pain	302,687
PTSD	269,556
Scars	218,910
Ankle injury	203,032
Migraine	168,415
Arthritis of spine	174,354
Sleep apnea	145,340
Hearing loss	146,429

1. Nearly half of all terror-war vets have already applied for disability, so the ultimate level of receiving benefits will eventually exceed that level.

Sources: Casualty Analysis System Defense (2017); Armed Forces Medical Surveillance Monthly Report (2012, 2013); DoD "Post-discharge Cause of Death Analysis" (2015); Congressional Research Service "A Guide to U.S. Military Casualty Statistics" (2015); V.A. "America's Wars" (2016); V.A. Annual Benefits Report (2015)

Mental Health

As in athletics, concussions are not uncommon in military life—with four out of five incidents taking place at U.S. bases rather than during deployments. Among recently deployed servicemembers, roadside bomb blasts and more routine events like vehicle accidents caused some concussions and some serious brain injuries. Post-traumatic stress diagnoses are rising for a variety of reasons. Compared to equivalent-age civilian counterparts, alcohol use is higher among servicemembers, and drug use is lower.

Total military concussions or brain injuries 2000-2016 (80% occurred in U.S., 20% during deployment)	
Severe concussion or brain injury	8,778
Moderate concussion	32,434
Mild concussion	294,010

Psychological and behavioral indicators			
	Deployed	Never deployed	Civilian Counterparts
War on terror veterans who experienced PTSD	2% to 17%	2% to 3%	4%
Active military who experienced depression at some point in career	13%	6%	16%
Active military using alcohol heavily within past 12 months	8%		5%
Active military using an illegal drug within the past month	~1%		22%
Active military misusing a prescription drug within the past month	~1%		6%
Annual suicides among servicemembers	475		
Increased risk of suicide for veterans compared to similar civilian population	21%		

Sources: DoD Defense and Veterans Brain Injury Center "Worldwide Numbers for TBI"; Frueh, Richardson and Acierno "Prevalence Estimates of Combat-Related PTSD: A Critical Review" (2010); Gadermann, Engel, et al. "Prevalence of DSM-IV Major Depression Among U.S. Military Personnel: Meta-analysis and simulation"; DoD "2011 Dept. of Defense Health-Related Behaviors Survey of Active Duty Military Personnel" (2013); SAMHSA, "Results from the 2011 National Survey on Drug Use and Health" (2012); V.A., "Suicide Among Veterans and Other Americans 2001-2014" (2016)

Family and Geography

Most veterans and servicemembers these days are married. Most veterans and many servicemembers are also responsible for children. The ratio of single parents in the military is vastly lower than in the civilian population. A very small fraction of households have dual military heads. Veterans are somewhat likelier to live in rural areas. All big states have lots of veterans.

Marital status of veterans and others				
	Married	Divorced	Widowed /separated	Never married
Veterans of war on terror	55%	14%	4%	27%
Other veterans	66%	16%	11%	7%
Non-veterans	48%	11%	8%	33%
Military personnel	51%	5%	~ 0%	43%

Dependents of active military	
Servicemembers with children	873,884 (41%)
Dependents of servicemembers by age	
0 to 11 1,210,668	
12 to 18 424,839	
Servicemembers who are single parents	133,555 (6%)
Servicemembers whose spouse is also military	47,273 (2%)

Veterans living in urban vs. rural areas		
	Urban	Rural
Overall U.S. population	84%	16%
Veterans of war on terror	74%	26%

States with largest populations of veterans	
Texas	1,755,680
California	1,670,186
Florida	1,533,306
Virginia	894,681
North Carolina	834,526
Georgia	830,089
New York	784,771
Pennsylvania	772,421
Ohio	751,763
Illinois	690,040

Sources: V.A. "Profile of Post 9/11 Veterans: 2014"; DoD "2015 Demographics: Profile of the Military Community," V.A. VetPop Model; V.A. "Characteristics of Rural Veterans: 2010"

Financial

Veterans, even the comparatively young men and women who served in the war on terror, earn substantially more than non-veterans. They also have access to special public benefits, in addition to what they earn. Veterans are thus much less likely to be poor, and comparatively few are homeless.

Median 2014 earnings full-time workers		
	Male	Female
Non-veterans	$467989	$37,965
Veterans of the war on terror	$49,032	$41,456
Other veterans	$527926	$44,945

Median 2014 income earnings plus public benefits, all work statuses		
Non-veterans	$27,297	$16,691
Veterans of the war on terror	$29,946	$397960
Other veterans	$34,981	$277934

Percent living in poverty in 2014		
Non-veterans	13%	16%
Veterans of the war on terror	8%	10%
All veterans	7%	9%

Number of homeless veterans 2016 point-in-time count
39,471

Sources: V.A. "Profile of Post 9/11 Veterans: 2014" (2016); V.A. "Profile of Veterans in Poverty: 2014" (2016); HUD "2016 PIT Estimate of Veteran Homelessness in the U.S."

RAPID EXPANSION OF THE **DEPARTMENT OF VETERANS AFFAIRS**

Over the last decade, there has been an enormous infusion of government spending and public employment on behalf of former and current members of the military. The Department of Veterans Affairs has been the fastest-expanding major part of the federal government, with its total employment rising 60 percent over the last decade and its total spending soaring to two and a half times its previous level.

Department of Veterans Affairs Budget and Full-time Employees

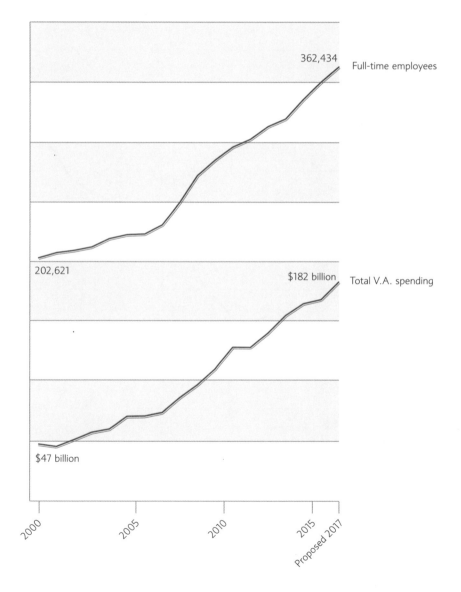

362,434 Full-time employees

202,621

$182 billion Total V.A. spending

$47 billion

2000   2005   2010   2015   Proposed 2017

Sources: V.A. Budget and Full-time Employees 2000-2012; Presidential Budget (2013-2017)

V.A. spending on medical care
(inflation-adjusted 2016 dollars)

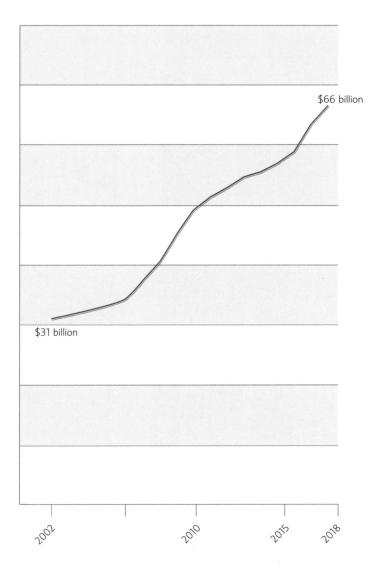

$66 billion

$31 billion

2002   2010   2015   2018

Sources: V.A. "Geographic Distribution of V.A. Expenditures"; Presidential Budget (2006-2017)

V.A. disability pay
(inflation-adjusted 2016 dollars)

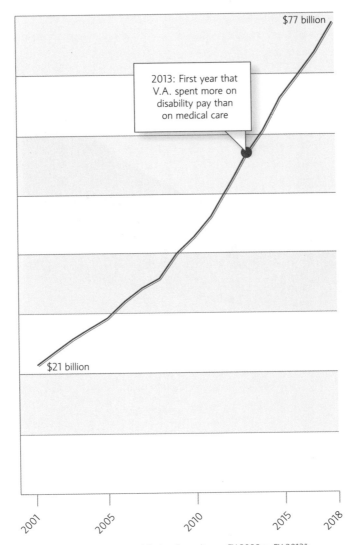

$77 billion

2013: First year that V.A. spent more on disability pay than on medical care

$21 billion

2001   2005   2010   2015   2018

Sources: V.A. "Disability Compensation and Patient Expenditures: FY 2000 to FY 2013"; Presidential Budget (2006-2017)

Veterans given high disability ratings

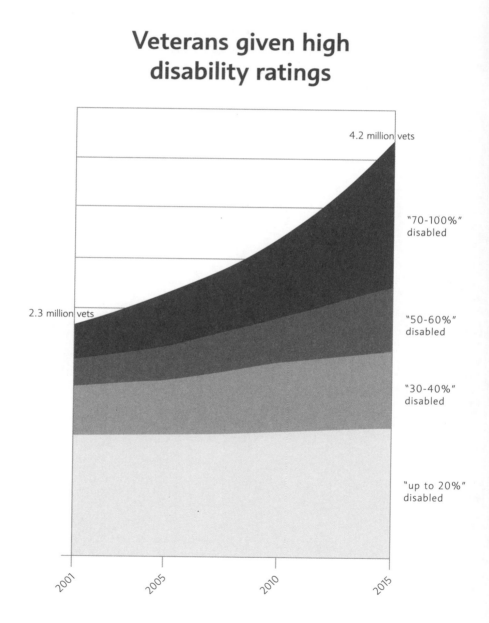

V.A. education-program users

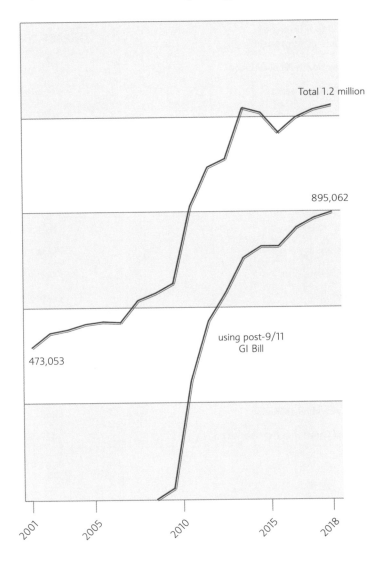

Total 1.2 million

895,062

473,053

using post-9/11
GI Bill

2001   2005   2010   2015   2018

Sources: V.A. "Education Program Beneficiaries FY2000 to FY2013"; Presidential Budget (2012-2017)

Federal spending on veterans

2016 Department of Veterans Affairs total	$167,484,033,000
Veterans Health Administration	$65,377,994,000
Health Care Services	$57,098,105,000
Rural health	$19,553,638,000
Mental health	$7,484,000,000
Special programs for terror-war vets	$5,025,900,000
Homeless programs	$1,477,000,000
Telehealth	$1,114,127,000
For caregivers	$622,466,000
Women veterans	$475,000,000
Traumatic brain injury	$271,800,000
Research	$1,891,860,000
Veterans Benefits Administration	$92,396,430,000
Disability compensation	$74,845,470,000
Pensions	$5,723,046,000
Education benefits	$12,941,285,000
Adaptive and rehabilitation	$1,641,810,000
National Cemeteries Administration	$271,220,000

continued on next page

Source: Presidential Budget FY2017

Veterans' funding from other agencies	
Department of Defense military retirement pay	$56,490,000,000
Department of Defense unemployment compensation	$537,107,000
Department of Labor veterans' employment and training	$271,110,000

Full-time employees at the Department of Veterans Affairs	349,800
Veterans Health Administration	311,232
Veterans Benefits Administration	21,871
National Cemeteries Administration	1,789

Facilities	
V.A. hospitals	144
Community living centers	136
Residential rehabilitation care facilities	120
Health-care centers	20
Community-based outpatient clinics	766
Vet centers	300

Sources: V.A. "Budget in Brief FY2017"; Presidential Budget FY2017

INDEX

ABOUT THE PHILANTHROPY ROUNDTABLE

The Philanthropy Roundtable is America's leading network of charitable donors working to strengthen our free society, uphold donor intent, and protect the freedom to give. Our members include individual philanthropists, families, corporations, and private foundations.

Mission

The Philanthropy Roundtable's mission is to foster excellence in philanthropy, to protect philanthropic freedom, to assist donors in achieving their philanthropic intent, and to help donors advance liberty, opportunity, and personal responsibility in America and abroad.

Principles

- Philanthropic freedom is essential to a free society
- A vibrant private sector generates the wealth that makes philanthropy possible
- Voluntary private action offers solutions to many of society's most pressing challenges
- Excellence in philanthropy is measured by results, not by good intentions
- A respect for donor intent is essential to long-term philanthropic success

Services

World-class conferences

The Philanthropy Roundtable connects you with other savvy donors. Held across the nation throughout the year, our meetings assemble grantmakers and experts to develop strategies for excellent local, state, and national giving. You will hear from innovators in K–12 education, economic opportunity, higher education, national security, and other fields. Our Annual Meeting is the Roundtable's flagship event, gathering the nation's most public-spirited and influential philanthropists for debates, how-to sessions, and discussions on the best ways for private individuals to achieve powerful results through their giving. The Annual Meeting is a stimulating and enjoyable way to meet principled donors seeking the breakthroughs that can solve our nation's greatest challenges.

Breakthrough groups
Our Breakthrough groups—focused program areas—build a critical mass of donors around a topic where dramatic results are within reach. Breakthrough groups become a springboard to help donors achieve lasting effects from their philanthropy. Our specialized staff of experts helps grantmakers invest with care in areas like anti-poverty work, philanthropy for veterans, and family reinforcement. The Roundtable's K–12 education program is our largest and longest-running Breakthrough group. This network helps donors zero in on today's most promising school reforms. We are the industry-leading convener for philanthropists seeking systemic improvements through competition and parental choice, administrative freedom and accountability, student-centered technology, enhanced teaching and school leadership, and high standards and expectations for students of all backgrounds. We foster productive collaboration among donors of varied ideological perspectives who are united by a devotion to educational excellence.

A powerful voice
The Roundtable's public-policy project, the Alliance for Charitable Reform (ACR), works to advance the principles and preserve the rights of private giving. ACR educates legislators and policymakers about the central role of charitable giving in American life and the crucial importance of protecting philanthropic freedom—the ability of individuals and private organizations to determine how and where to direct their charitable assets. Active in Washington, D.C., and in the states, ACR protects charitable giving, defends the diversity of charitable causes, and battles intrusive government regulation. We believe the capacity of private initiative to address national problems must not be burdened with costly or crippling constraints.

Protection of donor interests
The Philanthropy Roundtable is the leading force in American philanthropy to protect donor intent. Generous givers want assurance that their money will be used for the specific charitable aims and purposes they

believe in, not redirected to some other agenda. Unfortunately, donor intent is usually violated in increments, as foundation staff and trustees neglect or misconstrue the founder's values and drift into other purposes. Through education, practical guidance, legislative action, and individual consultation. The Philanthropy Roundtable is active in guarding donor intent. We are happy to advise you on steps you can take to ensure that your mission and goals are protected.

Must-read publications
Philanthropy, the Roundtable's quarterly magazine, is packed with useful and beautifully written real-life stories. It offers practical examples, inspiration, detailed information, history, and clear guidance on the differences between giving that is great and giving that disappoints.

We also publish a series of guidebooks that provide detailed information on the very best ways to be effective in particular aspects of philanthropy. These guidebooks are compact, brisk, and readable. Most focus on one particular area of giving—for instance, how to improve teaching, charter-school expansion, support for veterans, programs that get the poor into jobs, how to invest in public policy, and other topics of interest to grantmakers. Real-life examples, hard numbers, first-hand experiences of other donors, recent history, and policy guidance are presented to inform and inspire savvy donors.

The Roundtable's *Almanac of American Philanthropy* is the definitive reference book on private giving in our country. It profiles America's greatest givers (historic and current), describes the 1,000 most consequential philanthropic achievements since our founding, and compiles comprehensive statistics on the field. Our *Almanac* summarizes the major books, key articles, and most potent ideas animating U.S. philanthropy. It includes a 23-page timeline, national poll, legal analysis, and other crucial—and fascinating—finger-tip facts on this vital piece of American culture.

Join the Roundtable!

When working with The Philanthropy Roundtable, members are better equipped to achieve long-lasting success with their charitable giving. Your membership in the Roundtable will make you part of a potent network that understands philanthropy and strengthens our free society. Philanthropy Roundtable members range from Forbes 400 individual givers and the largest American foundations to small family foundations and donors just beginning their charitable careers. Our members include:

- Individuals and families
- Private foundations
- Community foundations
- Venture philanthropists
- Corporate giving programs
- Large operating foundations and charities that devote more than half of their budget to external grants

Philanthropists who contribute at least $100,000 annually to charitable causes are eligible to become members of the Roundtable and register for most of our programs. Roundtable events provide you with a solicitation-free environment.

For more information on The Philanthropy Roundtable or to learn about our individual program areas, please call (202) 822-8333 or e-mail main@PhilanthropyRoundtable.org.

ABOUT THE AUTHOR

Thomas Meyer is the program director for veterans services at The Philanthropy Roundtable, and co-founder of the Independence Project. He authored *Serving Those Who Served*, a 2013 guidebook to philanthropy for veterans, and has published articles in *Philanthropy* and *Security Studies*, and been quoted on this subject in the *New York Times* and elsewhere. Before joining the Roundtable, he completed research with U.S. and U.K. army officers focused on counterinsurgency work in Iraq and Afghanistan. He graduated with distinction in sociology from Yale University, and completed a Fox Fellowship at the University of Cambridge. Thomas grew up in an Army family and currently lives in Washington, D.C.